The Evolution of the Symphony Orchestra

History, Problems and Agendas

The Evolution of the Symphony Orchestra

A Conference
sponsored by the
Wheatland
Foundation
Chaired by
Isaac Stern

History, Problems and Agenda

Weidenfeld and Nicolson
London

Published in association with the
Wheatland Foundation by
George Weidenfeld and Nicolson Ltd
91 Clapham High St
London SW4 7TA

Typeset, printed and bound by
Butler & Tanner Ltd, Frome and London

ISBN 0 297 82032 X

Contents

The Evolution of the Symphony Orchestra: History, Problems and Agendas
A Wheatland Foundation Conference
Jerusalem, December 1986

List of Participants

RICHARD BAECHI (SWITZERLAND) Managing Director, Tonhalle Orchestra, Zurich. President, European Conference of Orchestras

ISAIAH BERLIN (U.K.) Teacher, Philosopher, and Musicologist

GARY BERTINI (ISRAEL) Conductor

CHRISTOPHER BISHOP (U.K.) Managing Director, London Philharmonia Orchestra

PIERRE BOULEZ (FRANCE) Composer, Conductor

ALFRED BRENDEL (U.K.) Pianist

HUMPHREY BURTON (U.K.) Executive Producer, Performing Arts, BBC Television

SEMYON BYCHKOV (U.S.A.) Conductor

PETER DIAMAND (U.S.A.) Conference Director, Artistic Advisor, Orchestre de Paris

HENRI DUTILLEUX (FRANCE) Composer

ERNEST FLEISCHMANN (U.S.A.) Executive Director, Los Angeles Philharmonic Orchestra Association

LAWRENCE FOSTER (U.S.A.) Conductor

CATHERINE FRENCH (U.S.A.) Conductor

ANN GETTY (U.S.A.) Publisher, Wheatland Foundation President

GORDON GETTY (U.S.A.) Composer, Patron of Arts

ALEXANDER GOEHR (U.K.) Composer, Conductor, Professor of Music and Fellow of Trinity Hall

PETER HEYWORTH (U.K.) Writer and Music Critic, the *Observer*

LILIAN HOCHHAUSER (U.K.) Concert Agent

HANS LANDESMANN (AUSTRIA) Artistic Director of the European Community Youth Orchestra

ANNA LINDAL (SWEDEN) Lead Violin, Stockholm Philharmonic Orchestra

FRANZ XAVER OHNESORG (F.R.G.) Director, Kölner Philharmonic

PETER PASTREICH (U.S.A.) Executive Director, San Francisco Symphony Orchestra

JOSEPH POLISI (U.S.A.) President, The Juilliard School, New York

HEIN VAN ROYEN (NETHERLANDS) Artistic Manager, Royal Concertgebouw Orchestra, Amsterdam

JOHN RUSHBY-SMITH (U.K.) Senior Music Studio Manager, BBC Radio

HANS ULRICH SCHMID (F.R.G.) Concert Agent

AVI SHOSHANI (ISRAEL) General Secretary, Israel Philharmonic Orchestra

MICHAL SMOIRA-COHN (ISRAEL) Head of Music, Israel Broadcasting Authority

NICHOLAS SNOWMAN (U.K.) General Director, Arts, South Bank Board, London

ISAAC STERN (U.S.A.) Violinist, President of Carnegie Hall

WOLFGANG STRESEMANN (F.R.G.) Former Director, Berlin Philharmonic Orchestra

JOSEPH TAL (ISRAEL) Composer

BASIL TSCHAIKOV (U.K.) Director, National Centre for Orchestral Studies, London

PIERRE VOZLINSKY (FRANCE) General Administrator, Orchestre de Paris

ALBERT K. WEBSTER (U.S.A.) Executive Vice President and Managing Director, New York Philharmonic Orchestra

GEORGE WEIDENFELD (U.K.) Publisher, Wheatland Foundation Chairman

KARSTEN WITT (F.R.G.) Director, German Philharmonic Youth Orchestra

FREDERICK ZENONE (U.S.A.) Cellist, National Symphony Orchestra, Former Chairperson of the International Conference of Symphony and Orchestra Musicians

Welcome

ANN GETTY: I am delighted to be in the company of so many professionals who have helped to make the orchestra what it is. But all people – professionals, amateurs, music lovers and even the tone-deaf – have a stake in its future. Man is a cultural animal. The Magdalenian paintings show him playing the flute. He has known music and painting longer than he has known farming and cities. He needs music, even without knowing why. Man is the animal that can distinguish the probable from the possible. Cities, for better or worse, are part of what is possible on earth, and music is a part of man's vision of what is possible in himself. I should like to turn the meeting over to George Weidenfeld, the chairman.

GEORGE WEIDENFELD: I am very pleased to be able to join Ann Getty in welcoming you on this occasion. At this conference, the guests need no introduction, but the hosts probably do. The Wheatland Foundation is a young institution: it's barely two years old. Set up to help literature and the performing arts internationally, its main function is to organize conferences to stimulate discussion on problems affecting those arts, not only to provide a clearing house for ideas but to act in concert with other foundations, philanthropic institutions and individuals to see that positive action arises from these discussions. We welcome participants in these conferences to come up, if possible, with not only thought-provoking and mind-clearing formulations, but with concrete resolutions that can be processed and worked on and, one hopes, funded.

We have had, so far, two rather successful conferences. The first, on the future of opera, took place in Venice in the summer of 1985. It bore tangible results, largely in the form of anonymous donations, but, above all, it cleared the air on a number of interesting problems. The magazine *Daedalus*, associated with the American Academy of Arts and Sciences, is this month publishing a summary of those proceedings as part of a special issue on opera. We also held an important conference on literary translation, at Leeds Castle last November. We are also organizing an international annual conference on world literature and a number of smaller conferences dealing with the problem of monitoring the new literature of other countries, which in turn links up with problems of translation.

I would like at this stage to thank Mayor Kollek and Mrs Cheshin, the director of the Jerusalem Foundation, who helped us greatly in organizing it. And now I would like to yield this microphone to the man who, having accepted a brief to organize this conference, made it happen: our conference director, Mr Peter Diamand.

PETER DIAMAND: Ladies and gentlemen, I would just like to say thank you and welcome. Thank you, in the first place, to the Wheatland Foundation which has arranged this conference; to Mrs Getty and Lord Weidenfeld and all those who have been so very helpful in the organizing of this meeting. Lord Weidenfeld already mentioned the Mayor of Jerusalem, Mr Kollek, and the Jerusalem Foundation. We are all particularly grateful to the Jerusalem Music Centre where we gather here; to Mr Ram Evron, its director; and to all those who have helped, both in London and in Jerusalem, in the preparation of this visit.

Unfortunately, some of our friends who had hoped to be with us had, for various reasons, to cancel their participation. These are Professor Altenburger, from the Vienna Philharmonic Orchestra; Luciano Berio, who, at the last moment, was prevented from joining us; Leonard Bernstein; Harrison Birtwistle; Joachim Kaiser; the French Minister for Culture, François Léotard, who had intended to be with us; Massimo Bogianchino, former director of La Scala and the Maggio Musicale and present Mayor of Florence; Professor Albert Moser; Dr Wolfgang Stresemann; Ronald Wilford from New York; and Claude Samuel from Paris. They all wished me to let you know how much they regret not being here and send their best wishes.

GEORGE WEIDENFELD: I now call on Isaac Stern, who has kindly agreed to be the chairman of the sessions.

ISAAC STERN: Welcome, ladies and gentlemen, to the Jerusalem Music Centre. The program of this conference, as you may have gathered if you've read through the agenda, is both long and comprehensive. It will be something of a task to make order out of so many possibilities. There are quite a few of us here, and I am sure we have not come all this distance to remain silent observers; everyone must and should have a say.

Feeling we should not predetermine which subjects get how much attention, from how many and at what length, we have set up a loose framework as a guide: starting with the introduction by Mr Peter Heyworth, seven or eight prepared papers will be delivered. After each of them, anybody who wishes to add to or to comment on what has just been said may contribute. None of this precludes the possibility that, later on in the conference, any other subject be raised or any subject in the prepared papers be brought back to the floor for further discussion.

As Lord Weidenfeld has said, the principal, if difficult, idea is to try to find answers to the various problems of this organism known as a symphony orchestra, so that useful efforts can be made to sustain its powers, to buttress its strength, to make it more effective wherever it may operate. Each of you will have a different view as to how this can be done. It will be interesting to see if, by the time the conference is over, the various views can meld into one useful basis for further thought and work, as we go on far beyond the limitations of these few days. I shall try my best to act fairly as chairman. I will listen with the greatest pleasure to anything that your accumulated wisdom and experience can bring us.

Introduction

PETER HEYWORTH: I was dismayed when Peter Diamand insisted that I introduce this seminar. Most of you, as conductors, composers, soloists, managers and impresarios, are in regular contact with orchestras. You certainly don't need a mere critic to tell you about their problems. I won't venture into the practical side of concert giving, but would like to glance at a few of the more deep-seated problems confronting the orchestra as an instrument today, perhaps even threatening its existence. These long-term issues get less attention than they deserve; it would be a pity if this conference failed to consider them. They may bring us onto controversial ground, but if anything I say helps to stir up discussion, it will have served its purpose.

I cannot believe that anyone would have sat around discussing the orchestra two hundred years ago. Haydn would have found the notion very odd. Even a century ago, it would have been hard to envisage such a gathering. What would there have been to talk about? To all intents and purposes, the orchestra was in robust health. Indeed, it was getting bigger and better every day. I suspect that one reason we are here today is that we are no longer quite so sure this is the case. Has the orchestra, perhaps, in the course of the second half of the twentieth century, begun to lose the sense of direction that drove it from one triumph to the next over a period of more than two hundred years?

Some voices will dispute this. Never before have so many people attended orchestral concerts; never before has the sound of orchestral music been so widely familiar. They can argue that just as music in the home was the basic experience of the nineteenth century, so the representative sound in the twentieth century is that of the symphony orchestra, not merely in concert halls but through TV, radio and records.

That's all true, but we shouldn't allow ourselves to be deceived by the mere proliferation of music that has taken place in the course of this century. Many empires have continued to expand on the periphery long after an inner sense of purpose had begun to fail. The great success enjoyed as a purveyor of music is no guarantee of the orchestra's health. The immense transformation undergone between the time of Haydn and the time of Mahler didn't come about by chance. Nor did it occur because new instruments had become available. What drove the orchestra forward during that period were the demands made of it by composers. Composers made the orchestra what it is today. Of course, social and economic factors also played their part, but basically it was the search of creators for new sounds and new fields of expression that pushed forward the frontiers of instrumental sound. Composers are indeed still doing that, but it seems to me that an essential change in the relationship between composer and orchestra has come about in the course of this century.

A hundred years ago, developments within the orchestra were part and parcel of developments in musical thinking. An obvious example: increasingly chromatic harmony called for increasingly elaborate instrumental textures. Creativity and the orchestra marched hand in hand. Can that still be said to be the case? I wonder. A taste for new instrumental combinations, new colors and textures, certainly reemerged with particular energy after 1945, perhaps in reaction to the rather puritanical world of *Die neue Sachlichkeit* between the two wars, but composers have increasingly sought those new combinations outside the framework of the traditional orchestra. They have turned to chamber ensembles of varying shapes and sizes. They have divided the orchestra into groups. Percussion has burst its narrow banks and grown to formerly inconceivable proportions. Electronic sounds have been introduced in growing profusion. Even composers who have remained faithful to the traditional orchestra have rarely accepted it as it stood. In short, composers in general are no longer ready to take the orchestra more or less as they find it. That represents a crucial change.

Although the orchestra was gradually being transformed throughout the nineteenth century, Verdi remained content at the end of his long life to write for an expanded version of the band used by Donizetti. Strauss composed for an enlarged Wagnerian orchestra. Until 1914 you could still expect to find most of the usual players in their accustomed places on the platform, whether they were playing music by Rimsky-Korsakov or Schoenberg. Today the orchestra, in so far as it continues to meet composers' demands, is a chameleon. It changes shape and size continually. Composers take from it what they want, drop what they don't need and frequently add individual requirements which are liable to alter from work to work. As far as new music is concerned, the orchestra is in danger of losing its identity, becoming merely an ad hoc assembly of instruments.

Does that matter? Plainly, some think it doesn't. In their view, if contemporary composers withdraw from the orchestra as it has been handed down to them, that's their lookout. But that may prove a shortsighted view. Many orchestras can and do survive while playing little new music worthy of the name, but in the long run they will pay dearly for immuring themselves in the status quo. In doing so, they deprive themselves of the very creative forces that have given the orchestra life over the past two centuries. It would be a mistake to suppose that this growing gulf between creativity and the orchestra is confined to the field of new music – dangerous though that is. Creation and re-creation are closely linked. Interpretation stems from creativity and changes as creativity does.

Arthur Nikisch was in his time regarded as the very epitome of the great conductor. Today the recording he made of Beethoven's Fifth Symphony, in 1921, is hard to listen to, so indulgent are the tempo changes. What has altered our view of Beethoven so drastically? For a large part, the experience of the new music that lies between the time of Nikisch and our own. Had Otto Klemperer not been deeply immersed in the music of Stravinsky and the new classicism in the twenties, he would hardly have arrived at what was regarded in its rigor as a revolutionary interpretation of Beethoven. Conversely, the very different spirit of Furtwängler's performances of Beethoven reflects the durability of his late-Romantic loyalties. And the impact of creativity on interpretation must have been even more immediate in an earlier period. Strauss and Mahler, not to mention Wagner, were both conductors as well as composers. Who can doubt today that Boulez's approach to Debussy is not deeply impregnated by his own music? This intimate link between creativity and interpretation has become much rarer today. As a result, conducting is increasingly a matter of mere virtuosity. Not for nothing has Herbert von Karajan come to be regarded as the representative conductor of our time. Technical perfection has become an end in itself.

This brings me to what I see as the baleful influence of the recording industry. Until the last war, orchestras existed to give concerts, and those concerts provided them with their living. Occasional recordings represented no more than the icing on the gingerbread. Today, however, the system has been inverted. Orchestras engage artists and plan programs with one eye on a recording contract. Indeed, meeting those requirements, since recording companies exist to make profits, sometimes works against innovation and weakens the links between the orchestra and new music. These pressures impose an ossification, institutionalizing the orchestra's growing remoteness from the creative pressures that once made it a living entity. What is not growing is dying.

In the absence of creativity, the concert is reduced to the level of a circus act. Who has not experienced one of those evenings when one seems to be attending the concert of the recording? Audiences may continue to cheer, sales of recordings may increase, but am I alone in sensing an inner deadness of spirit? The recent and growing demand for historical recordings, regardless of their technical shortcomings, may be a straw in the wind here; it suggests an increasing dissatisfaction with the glib, lacquered performances that loom so large today.

Indications of the growing gulf between creativity and the orchestra extend far beyond the field of new music – which, contrary to what is often supposed, can survive better without the orchestra than the orchestra can without it. At the other end of the time scale, the orchestra is in the process of losing its grip on the pre-Classical repertoire. Here, as in the contemporary field, small groups have proved more responsive to new needs, in this case to new modes of interpreting early music. There are even signs of dissatisfaction within the orchestra, on the part of musicians themselves. A growing number of young instrumentalists, often among the most talented, are disenchanted with the orchestral treadmill, finding it more rewarding to work with a variety of small groups.

Is the present-day orchestra an obsolescent instrument? Its predicament seems to lie in confronting a need for change at a time when its own narrow views of its functions, together with pressures from the recording industry on which it so largely depends, have caused it to turn its back on the future. A new flexibility, a new responsiveness to new developments, is needed at a moment when the orchestra is a prisoner of tradition.

PIERRE BOULEZ: Although confronted with these problems every day, I don't think that they belong to our period alone. If you read Berlioz's commentaries on the orchestras of his time, or Schumann's commentaries, you see the same problems.

Debussy, speaking of the orchestra in Paris, complained about conventional programming and bad rehearsing. And the stupidity of the audience, if I may say so, is always the same. The problem isn't really any worse than it was before. On the contrary, many things have improved. Rehearsal conditions fifty years ago or a hundred years ago were appalling compared to those we have now, when a minimum of rehearsals for a concert is four or five. In Debussy's time, you had one or two rehearsals, and that was it. If you consider that Schoenberg's Five Orchestral Pieces were played in London before the First World War after one rehearsal, which included the rest of the program, you cannot imagine how these pieces were performed! We must not blame our period for the conditions provided.

The recording industry is very conventional in the main – although we cannot really blame them for trying to make money – but recordings have also set new, higher standards in performance. While listening to a mediocre performance, the recording made by a very good orchestra is in your ear. Mediocre performances are still possible, but now you know that they are mediocre. Or imagine living in the city where I was born: seven thousand inhabitants, no orchestra, no chorus, nothing. One relies completely on the recording industry, which has brought a whole culture into being, a repertoire which would not otherwise be heard.

One reason for the general discontent with orchestral life is the lack of flexibility. In the nineteenth century, everything was standardized. The number of instruments we can have is fixed. You may want to perform Schoenberg's op. 22, which requires seven clarinets, so you must pay for two or three – where would you find seven clarinets in the orchestra? Statistically, within the repertoire you have to have a certain number of instruments. Beyond this limit, you pay extra instrumentalists who cannot be included in the corpus of musicians. There is a conflict between the economic optimum and your desire for an unlimited number of instruments.

Also, composers nowadays want different orchestral configurations. What happens? People who have played together for years, who are accustomed to being near to each other and hearing each other, are absolutely disoriented when they suddenly hear, instead of the flute just behind them, a trumpet in front of them. Their whole environment is changed. Perhaps if their education had been more adventurous we would have fewer problems of this order. But this cannot be solved by discussion. We confront a reluctance that is enforced by the weight of tradition.

The orchestra should be an ensemble of possibilities, and not exclude anything; the repertoire however is becoming narrower and narrower. Much of it is being given to specialized groups, while the orchestra itself becomes like a museum, with a room for classical works and a room for contemporary works. The repertoire of a standard orchestra no longer touches the eighteenth century; that music is played on authentic instruments, or by those who have the so-called right style. The problems are very great. A musician in the orchestra cannot specialize in eighteenth-century music, in Baroque music, while playing it only three times a year. The same thing goes for contemporary music.

At present, if you want to organize the season as a series of concerts, you put in a little bit of salt, a little bit of pepper, a little bit of sugar; you make ten packages of this kind or twenty of that, and you sell them. This notion will progressively disappear; more and more, we have contrasts between concerts that are a mixture of pieces in different styles. We also have to capture people's attention for a specific period of time, both multiplying the type of concerts and holding strong, special events.

At the same time, we must create new environments for concerts. Normally, the house is opened at eight and closed at ten. People come and go; you don't try to keep an audience beyond those limits. It would be wise to create a place where people can come, for instance, at six, when they leave their offices. Somewhere they can not only eat – of course they must eat – but also obtain documentation, hear lectures, see films and be confirmed in their wish to hear something, have a chance to orient themselves and gain more information.

The future life of orchestras lies here, in greater flexibility of events and the creation of environments that induce people to listen to music. In this direction we have a lot to do, but I am not at all pessimistic. We are in a time of evolution and must follow this evolution in music – that's all. In theory, the problem is very simple, but very complex to solve day after day.

PETER HEYWORTH: Mr Boulez rightly says that Berlioz and Schumann were also discontented with the condition of the orchestra in their time, but in their efforts to ameliorate that situation, they pushed for a bigger and better orchestra. Composers now are disrupting the traditional symphony orchestra – we are facing a very different situation.

ISAAC STERN: Mr Heyworth and Mr Boulez have referred to the orchestra, you will have noticed, from two slightly different points of view. Mr Heyworth was possibly influenced by the manner in which the orchestra performs, lives and operates in England; Mr Boulez has a worldwide experience, but has also spent many years with an orchestra that has a regular subscription, many repeats of the performances and so on. This brings us to the question of how we describe the animal that we are trying to define. What are the orchestra's geographic, demographic, political differences in various parts of the world? To what degree do questions posed today fit all of them, or some of them part of the time, or perhaps some of them none of the time?

ERNEST FLEISCHMANN: Mr Heyworth and Mr Boulez have laid out the problem and even given us some solutions; we can almost go home. However, in between the problem and its solution are a number of practical issues. Both of them pointed to a kind of schizophrenia in the orchestra, namely that it is essentially a fixed, nineteenth-century body. Mr Heyworth referred to the orchestra as losing its identity, dividing into smaller groups in order to play new music, while the music of the Classical and Baroque eras, because of all we now know of performing styles and so on, is probably no longer possible for the orchestra as such. Mr Boulez has asked us to be more flexible, to provide events in environments that will allow the orchestra to flourish.

With the improvement in both playing standards and the musical, intellectual capacities of younger musicians, surely it is possible to gain a new identity by being flexible, presenting concerts with small groups, with musicians who specialize in early music and so on. The schizophrenia exists in the purpose of today's orchestra. Are we entertainers? The growth in our audiences is not a growth in quality, it's a growth in people who expect entertainment – an audience that the orchestra has created. The one-rehearsal concert which Mr Boulez speaks of is still prevalent, except – thank goodness – they don't have to do Schoenberg's op. 16 with only one rehearsal. But it's just as difficult to play a Beethoven symphony well with that preparation as it is to play Schoenberg. How do we justify our existence? We talk about the Rachmaninov, Beethoven, Tchaikovsky programs. Our big task is to achieve what Mr Boulez has postulated: to educate the audiences, not only children but the very large audiences that come to our concerts in the evenings; to get that audience to demand flexibility. Some of us are doing that already. The subscription system is beautifully designed for that: we can give subscribers virtually anything, provided we give them reasons for it, provided indeed we create an environment where they can come earlier and learn about what they are going to hear – even if it isn't the same soup with the same pepper, the same salt and the same sugar that they've had for years.

If we can prepare our audiences with a wider range of programming, if we can stop audiences complaining that one of the pieces is played by seventeen instruments when they've paid for a hundred, we have an incredible world ahead of us. We have an incredible future just because things are changing, just because composers, who became skeptical over the last thirty or forty years about getting performances from orchestras, are writing for smaller ensembles. The orchestras themselves contain those ensembles. An orchestra that is afraid of paying for an extra two clarinets in order to play a worthwhile piece of music should put another five cents on the ticket price next season: it can pay for an extra hundred clarinets. It's all a matter of proportion. I hope we will concern ourselves with audience education in order to create the kind of quality audience that is represented now by the quantity audience to whom we play.

BASIL TSCHAIKOV: So far, the remarks that have been made, referring to the orchestra, have been made in the way that we usually speak about England, or the Government, or Marks & Spencer – but of course an orchestra is made up of human beings, each one of whom has aspirations and intentions and is a product of a time, an environment, a nation. As someone who has spent forty years playing in one or other of the London orchestras, I may perhaps speak with some experience of the great changes that have taken place in the musicians' attitudes.

It is an unusual thing for an orchestral player to find himself in complete agreement with a critic, but Mr Heyworth's comments seemed to me a profound, concise outlining of the situation. As has been said, the orchestra, in the shape that we have it now, is essentially a nineteenth-century institution, but of course it goes back much further. At the beginning of this symposium, I heard the expression 'symphony orchestra.' When did people first say 'symphony orchestra' as detached from any other sort of orchestra, group of players or ensemble? It happens to be a rather large ensemble. Perhaps that's its biggest problem, because every player starts off on an ego trip. The whole of the material that we learned to play our instruments on, whether the clarinet, violin or trombone, is essentially solo material. And yet, the more successful we are as instrumentalists, the more we have to sublimate our individuality, not only to the needs of playing with a very large group of people but also – I say this with great trepidation, yet it reflects the attitude of most musicians – to the tyranny of the conductor. Now, by tyranny I do not mean that they ill-treat or are harmful to the musicians, but that players in an orchestra have to submit, instant by instant, to the dictates of a single individual, about music to which each of them has intense, personal responses, is a tremendous burden. I see only one other person here – Miss Lindal – who will know what it is like to sit perhaps five days a week, forty-five or forty-eight weeks a year, six hours a day, while every movement you make, in the music that is the substance of your being, is dictated to you by others.

In the past, postmen wore their uniform, as did railwaymen, porters or engine drivers, with pride. Now you can't get bus conductors or postmen to wear a uniform. People were able to say 'Good morning, sir' without feeling that they were diminishing themselves and losing dignity. There have been enormous changes in social relations, and yet we expect young musicians, who have had a totally different upbringing and education in a very different society, to behave as people did fifty or a hundred years ago. Of course, some things have not changed. A degree of frustration, which often shows itself in bizarre and unacceptable behavior on the part of players, remains: resistance to conductors, resistance to rehearsing something played many times before. Why have we got to have another three days' rehearsal on the Unfinished Symphony, which we've played for the last thirty years? All sorts of distortions take place because the environment in which they work is unsatisfactory. As has been pointed out, the orchestra is becoming increasingly narrow.

In my lifetime, the repertoire for an orchestral player has very greatly diminished. In my three weeks' trial period in the London Philharmonic in 1943, I played a more varied set of programs than most orchestral musicians in London would now play in the course of three or four months. That's an important element in the future of the orchestra. Another is that performances have become stereotyped. The very high standards referred to, and the increasingly good recordings, do indeed exist. However, more and more frequently among the young musicians who come to play to me, I hear that virtuosity is commonplace, but music is increasingly rare. In the past, one heard bad intonation, not a good sound, an insecure rhythm, but somewhere, in among the cracks, one did hear people who liked music. Now one hears a lovely sound, one hears beautiful intonation, perfect articulation and technique, but no music in between it at all.

Most people these days have been brought up since babyhood on recordings. If all the people who listened to music went to concert halls, the orchestra wouldn't have any economic problems. But most people listen to music in a recorded form. However good it is, even the recording of a live performance, when you hear it for the second time you are hearing something which is the same as you heard it the first time. There is nothing else in our whole human life which is like that. Imagine if we made love in exactly the same way because it was marvelous once and we were condemned to do it like that for the rest of our lives. For that is what we do with a marvelous performance: we hear one performance of a work, we love it and we hear it over and over again. Our expectations are of what we heard before.

All these forces are at work to make the orchestra vulnerable to young musicians, the most serious, the most adventurous among them, not because they don't want to play serious music but because they don't want to condemn themselves to playing one sort of music all the time. The orchestra might become a resource center, rather than an instrument to play one sort of music. Musicians are educated enough now to consider playing many different sorts of music.

ERNEST FLEISCHMANN: Based on what Mr Tschaikov said, it is up to us who run the orchestras to make the lives of our musicians as musically interesting as possible. The more successful we are – taking for granted that economic conditions are now, by and large, more reasonable than they have ever been – the better the performances in the end, and the more chance we have of attracting that remarkable talent. Yes, they do play their instruments extremely well, but it's up to us to help broaden their musical horizons. And it's up to conductors, many of whom have derived from that scourge, the phonograph record, ideas of how to approach a piece. Conductors need to challenge musicians more. To play between the cracks, to take more risks and not to have one ear always on that recorded perfection that they think audiences need. An audience needs to be taken aback by an odd clarinet solo, which can make a concert. It needs to be taken aback by that difference, that quickening of the heart and pulse that a soloist in an orchestra can still achieve. We need to do more to give musicians the opportunity to take risks.

ALEXANDER GOEHR: Pierre Boulez was probably right to detect and, by implication, criticize a faint apocalyptic tone in Peter Heyworth's opening remarks. Indeed, many things are better now than they were in the past, even within our living memory. Certain technical aspects of music have improved. But one should not entirely ignore the central complaint offered in Mr Heyworth's slightly somber opening to this session, which has been reflected in Mr Tschaikov's statement.

A general belief appears that we have, on the one hand, a decaying center and on the other hand a need for 'flexibility' and an opening out into various regions. To add one element to this: there is such a thing as a classical canon on which the orchestra has been based in its nineteenth-century and early twentieth-century evolution. It isn't quite right to imply that the public is merely narrow-minded, as if this were 1899 and we were aesthetes attacking the public's conservatism. The public makes demands on the classical orchestra which, to some extent, it does not find fulfilled: that is, for a living cultivation of the classical canon. The danger is that flexibility, alteration of formula, will not specifically aid in performing that central function. The orchestra has survived in the past because the very great conductors, who were not only stick-waggers and tyrants but also musical thinkers, contributed something new. That classical canon must be cultivated if the orchestra is to survive, cultivated as a living thing and not merely as a homage, played in the first bit of the concert before some new alleged development takes place.

If it were to be agreed that the central purpose of the orchestra today is the defense of that classical canon, then what is new is a crucial issue. We can all visualize the orchestra existing as a museum to the total exclusion of new music. If contemporary music is to be included in the orchestra's work, this involves not only technical changes, the education of the audience and of other kinds of players, but the temptation of a sense of confrontation. The great achievements, on which we base our views of contemporary music, which were accomplished in the earlier part of the century, existed in a spirit of confrontation. The confrontations may have been based on rotten performances, no doubt they were, and they may not have aspired to particularly high standards, but some message was conveyed when Stravinsky or Schoenberg or Fauré was represented in public. That confrontation is an accurate, creative force, which will not be defended by a tech-nologically inspired educational procedure. Such an education would accustom the public to what it was about to receive, teaching an uncritical ear. We ought to take into account the traditional ear of the audience that goes to the symphony concert, and not simply throw it out as a retrogressive function with no particular point.

PIERRE BOULEZ: Musicians may be more tyrannical among themselves than the conductor is with musicians. Inside the orchestra, there is a hierarchy of musicians, which they them-selves support; a first clarinet finds it demeaning to go down to third clarinet. The Paris Opera ensemble abolished hierarchy: anyone could play anything. There were three violins – not a first or a second or a third; each played first when necessary. Within a group, the problem can be solved. Young people admitted into the orchestra at the eighth desk of the second group may wait ten or fifteen years to move to the third desk and have something more interesting to play. These young people must not be discouraged from playing a more prominent part in the orchestra. In New York, we employed the rotation system, meant to bring some movement among the strings. At the beginning, we tried rotation of the musicians one by one: the desks were absolutely disorganized. You had no sound anymore. It was a problem of democracy in opposition to hierarchy – a typical situation within the orchestra. We then tried to institute hierarchy within democracy, with the Ferris wheel solution, moving groups of musicians. Then there was cohesion without the absolute immobility which had been the rule before.

When you discard hierarchy, you discard a very strong principle, but also open a door for all the combinations we want to have – chamber groups, for instance. Chamber music should be an important part of the musician's life within the orchestra. One hears it said that chamber music is very good but that it is ultimately only chamber music. Not at all. The musician's experience of smaller ensembles enhances his con-tribution to the orchestra; the style and level of orchestral playing is improved enormously by this back and forth. If we want to discuss something very important in the orchestra's future, we have to speak first about hierarchy.

GARY BERTINI: What emerges is the importance of defining exactly what we mean when we say 'orchestra.' Different questions, problems and solutions are linked to that definition. Mr Tschaikov spoke of the orchestra in London; increased limitations in repertoire, for example, don't apply exactly the same way in different places in the world. Subsidized, radio, freelance, and half-freelance orchestras, the London type of orchestra, self-governed orchestras – they don't all have exactly the same problems.

More and more different types of orchestras have developed over the last twenty years: orchestras formed according to style or instruments, the Baroque-type orchestra, the reconstructed orchestras that link themselves to a certain style of playing based on an absolutely puritanical adherence to the middle road, which may lead to extremes. All of this, which includes the question of the number of rehearsals as it varies in the different types of orchestras and in those whose social organization is different, is relevant to our discussion.

The question of chamber music or smaller groups within a larger orchestra plays a large role at the moment in the life of an individual musician, the one frustrated sitting at desk eight number two. After his six hours are over, along with five of his friends, who have all chosen each other, he will play chamber music just the way he wants. This does not apply only to quintets, quartets or trios, but to larger groups. It's not new that many musicians who play second clarinet, or second violin or cello in an orchestra, also have their own groups where they conduct, or lead, or play in a different role. We have to enlarge as well on relationships within the circle of composer, performer, public. Composers do create or influence the development of the orchestra – but we speak of educating the public too. We should clarify what we mean by education. The word *event* is much stronger and has greater influence when we speak of our role as performing, rather than as a direct function of education.

One last point. We shouldn't forget that the social conditions of orchestral musicians in our time have changed to such an extent that the unions impose rules of how to work. This, together with the question of economics, plays a considerable role in musicians' lives today.

PIERRE VOZLINSKY: There is something of a more mechanical

nature which has not yet been discussed among us here: the dialectic between the conductor and the orchestra has fundamentally changed. Before the Second World War, what the conductor expected from the orchestra was paramount; now those responsible for managing orchestras know that what is important is what the orchestra expects from the conductor. The collective opinion has become of considerable importance. It is practically impossible to impose an unacceptable conductor on the musicians.

We live in a time of violent contradiction between the symphony orchestra, as one of the most complex collective activities executed by human beings, and musicians' very strong sense of individuality. An orchestra recently asked me to sign what we call in France *le bon à tirer*: in other words, the green light to manufacture recordings. This approval was to be individually signed by each musician participating in the recording! Consider the consequences of this attitude. Any conductor would consider it an insult. This describes a situation that, in a country such as mine, is particularly intense. A nineteenth-century journalist said that France has fifty million inhabitants and as many malcontents. The orchestra used to be a cross between a group of domestic servants and a military platoon, but musicians no longer consider themselves either servants or soldiers. From a purely functional point of view, this heightened individualism is a serious problem in the symphony orchestra.

ISAAC STERN: Mr Vozlinsky has begun to touch on the subject of national differences between orchestras, their identity, their recognition of themselves. The problems so far enunciated would perhaps appear familiar to all groups known as orchestras no matter where they are. Would anyone like to elucidate further the national differences that affect the orchestra as we know it?

FREDERICK ZENONE: Only to the extent that differences between orchestras have a bearing on the solution Mr Boulez has proposed. The freelance orchestra brings back into the orchestra an entire experience from beyond it, although in some parts of the world, the freelance orchestra may be so preoccupied with survival that it has no time to bring that experience back in. But in the salaried orchestra, the problem is even more acute: we try to perpetuate this thing called the orchestra by reinventing our history.

What is wrong with orchestras now – that they are paralyzed, calcified, ossified – and the problems of the audience are the same. We continue to try to reinvent the nineteenth-century orchestra and to solve our twentieth- and twenty-first-century problems as we believe they might have been solved then. I don't know of many orchestras in which musicians think of themselves – I speak as an orchestral musician – as a community of musicians. In our private moments, we must lament that there are few communities of 105, 110 musicians who remain musically curious over a thirty-year orchestral career. As we became institutions, it seems we became so preoccupied with survival that we forgot to pay attention. And that's what we need to do: feed that community.

One problem with contemporary music in orchestras is that we expect everybody to be current – and all at the same time. In fact, five years after leaving music school, you're already 'old stuff.' You don't understand very much anymore. The kids coming out of music school are much more *au fait* than anyone sitting in a symphony orchestra. The curiosity that exists with smaller groups, the performance opportunities they have, the chamber music possibilities, are all contained in the idea of orchestral community. Perhaps these could be brought back into the orchestra. Instead of always trying to reinvent on the grand scale, we would have something that lives.

Some of the same problems might be solved by looking in the same way at the community of the audience. In America if one were to ask the musicians, 'What is this community, who are these people that you play for?' you would get very strange answers. Very limited answers. That orchestra, with few exceptions, does not feel a part of the community.

NICHOLAS SNOWMAN: It is sometimes useful to place the orchestra within a general artistic context. When musical activity can take place in counterpoint to other artistic fields, whether cinema, painting or theatre, everything becomes distanced: the musician doesn't feel he's in his own little world.

Comparisons begin to be made. One hopes the audience, crossing from one endeavor to another, will be enlarged both intellectually and in numbers. This is the gamble, at least. The Pompidou Center has proved it can be a successful one. The Corbusier exhibition, for example, which is taking place in France and will travel to London, will be counterpointed with concerts of electronic music of Varèse, Krenek, etc. – which many musicians are very pleased to take part in.

The new musician, as we've said, will want to play Baroque music one day and contemporary music another, as well as take part in the symphony orchestra. Perhaps the new musician also goes to museums, reads books, is interested in things other than being on a production line, producing the same old symphonies, the same old works; therein may lie help for the future in general.

In London on the South Bank, we now have an education department, with a considerable budget, that never existed there before. That department is addressing itself not simply to a middle-class, white, privileged audience, but trying to bring in the local communities as well. That's important for changing the perception of the symphony concert, given the symphony audience and the subscription series that we know so well. Let's enlarge the discussion and not just keep it within the music field.

PETER PASTREICH: Mr Heyworth started by saying that a conference like this would have been unthinkable in Haydn's time and concluded that orchestras were healthier then. I think I would disagree: they simply weren't institutionalized then. Composers originally created the institution; as the nineteenth and twentieth centuries progressed, it became more complex, requiring an infrastructure of management, of music critics, press, musicians' unions and organizations of conservatories. That infrastructure of boards of directors, once created, had vested interest in perpetuating the orchestra.

We talk about continuing this institution at all costs, whether or not it continues to serve a function. We need to talk about ways to create a financial security that will permit us to address the real issues of our future. Financial security just piled on to keep us doing what we're doing, however, isn't going to solve basic problems. It needs to be related to the attainment of decentralization and, particularly, flexibility. We live in societies where there's an inappropriate allocation of resources. If in some way we could get beyond the issue of survival, we might better address these vital issues.

KARSTEN WITT: We listened just now to two different perspectives, one after the other: that of the musician, who sees the orchestra as a society in itself, and that of the concert hall manager, for whom the symphony orchestra is just a specialized group among others performing at his hall. An orchestra may be so far institutionalized that it becomes a society on its own; the interesting point is where the orchestra's structure influences its possible achievements. To make orchestras more appropriate to our societies' cultural needs, this structure must be changed, perhaps by considering the orchestra as a community.

In some orchestras the individual musician, unable to realize that a certain task can be interesting, used to playing a particular role and not thinking about it, does not want to change anything connected with his role. The position of the individual musician within the orchestra must change radically, making the orchestra not only a community functioning alone, but a community of interpreters who have a certain responsibility towards the composer and towards the public. Musicians might see that they are themselves part of the public and consider what is exciting for them as a part of that public. Before speaking about what the public demands nowadays, one must think that a very large part of the possible public – the society which is not within the concert halls – listens to recordings out of the orchestral repertoire and never goes to a symphony concert. This is especially true of young people; they can only be reached if you go to them, change the type of event and alter the repertoire.

PIERRE BOULEZ: We speak of the orchestra, and about education, but we haven't discussed our own system of education. Especially for strings, education at the conservatories is geared to a solo career. When you hold auditions for an orchestra, the young musicians play, for instance, the

Tchaikovsky concerto very quickly and very well – without much musicality, but well enough. But give them two lines of Bartók to sight-read, and they are lost. Even the most brilliant talent goes to pieces. The repertoire taught at the conservatory in Paris stopped with Debussy and Ravel. People open to new ideas at the beginning finished their studies completely closed. Another result of this type of education is that the musicians consider the orchestral profession a failure. There is no sense of collective effort, which is so important. To have education go beyond learning the instrument for a possible solo career is essential.

ERNEST FLEISCHMANN: I find three points raised of tremendous concern. First may I say in response to Mr Zenone, that in many orchestras the most severe problems exist not between musicians and management but between musicians and musicians. Mr Snowman's concern to address an audience larger than the middle-class one to which we are accustomed is enormously important. In Southern California, we're facing a significant change in population; in the next fifteen years our Hispanic and Asian audience will probably grow to out-number the white-Anglo and black audiences. Few of us have given any thought to these demographic changes, which affect European populations as well, or changes in age, class and education of our audiences.

Thirdly, Mr Pastreich's very pertinent point: we're so concerned about financial survival that we seem unable to pay the attention due our future artistic philosophies. Tremendous changes are taking place in the funding of all we are trying to do. We may construct here an ideal musical world, but we face greater financial pressures than ever before.

ISAAC STERN: Let me exercise the prerogative of the chair by making a few observations. I have, perhaps, had as much experience with orchestras as any of you, because I've been playing with orchestras for fifty years. It's a long time, and I have observed a number of changes. Much of what I see today disturbs me.

When I was growing up in San Francisco, I remember very well that a member of the San Francisco Symphony was a person in town, someone of importance – remember this was before they had what today amounts to a guaranteed annual wage, the fifty-two week season. The musician felt that he was recognized. In talking about the needs of the orchestral player and the problem of the conductor, we're skirting this issue. A musician needs certain things: he wants to have the respect and affection of the community around him; most of all, he wants to feel needed and useful. This element is most important to anyone making music. Additionally, nobody took up the point, at least in any depth, that the performance of the great repertoire we have inherited, that has made us musicians, is a repertoire unknown to enormously growing numbers of young people, even though, because of the great expansions of communications, each generation is increasingly aware of music.

There are several anomalies at work. We are talking about what is, in truth, an élite form of society. Élite not in the economic or social sense, but as it recognizes man's potential in a climate of popularism. That creates a certain problem. Then again, the enormous growth of the number of orchestras. Their qualities vary, naturally, but the numbers are impressive. What has gone by the board is that the pressure of constantly getting out what the marketing people call a 'product' begins to make the performer feel like a machine cog, and scream out for his rights as an individual.

Have you ever really forgotten the thrill of hearing a very great performance of Mozart or Beethoven? As Pierre Boulez said very clearly, these kids come out playing Tchaikovsky; you put up a Bartók, and they instantly get lost. Well, I submit to you that if you asked them to play two measures of Mozart properly, they would get equally lost. They don't know that either. This magic of what makes music – not the notes that are written but how you get from one note to another, and why you do that, and the enormous numbers of possibilities of doing it beautifully ... all of them are correct. How do you decide? Where do you go?

How do we continue that sense of enquiry, of personal excitement that seems to get so dreadfully dulled when the young people leave school and have to get into real life? Another problem of education: the real life as against the

imagined life; the true role of the history of music and of
musical performance, and how it has of necessity become an
evolutionary form that answers to the possibilities for the
instrument today; what is expected today of a young performer,
compared to the young performer fifty years ago. I'm not
speaking now of soloists. Certainly, you have touched on points
in education; we should follow that. You have touched on the
players' psyche, and we should follow that. Points have been
raised about the make-up of the coordinating or regulating
arm of the orchestra – the managers, the board of directors –
those should be followed to some degree. But they are all to be
followed for a reason. What is the ultimate reason? The making
of music. If we limit ourselves to observations that take in only
the changes of the last thirty or forty years, we do not recognize
the history of that change and the enormous wealth of creativity in music from 1895 to 1935.

When one uses the word 'contemporary,' what is meant?
That which was written last week, last month, last year or in
the last six years? All these things have to be discussed in
perspective – where the music came from in the first place and
why it does not always remain alive in performance today.
Only last month, I had the dismaying experience of playing
very well-known classic works – with one of the best, most
renowned, most highly praised musical organizations in the
United States – and finding it so difficult for the orchestra to
make music from one phrase to another that it was finally
impossible even to discuss the continuation of a recording. A
week later, in Japan, with a group of young kids from Tokyo
University, none of them over nineteen years old, I made the
recording with such pleasure, with such ease. There was an
enthusiasm, a love, a dedication and a willingness – a willingness to concede to a central idea, without which there can
be no concerted music-making. Chamber music is the greatest
teacher of this. As every musician of quality knows, if you can
play chamber music well, you can play anything: it's the rules
and the give-and-take of the chamber music discipline that are
so valuable.

All these things must be taken into consideration. It is not
my place, as chairman, to discuss where the answers lie. That
is your collective responsibility, but I should like to point you

a little further along those lines, and see what you can make of them. Now, let us continue with Mr Polisi on the subject of education in the United States.

Education

JOSEPH POLISI: Education is in fact an afterthought with reference to the orchestral experience, although sometimes blamed for the psychological and musical shortfalls of orchestra members. There is a gap in understanding between the educational process and the realization of professional goals. Any one of us is involved in educating young people about what it is to be an orchestral musician, not only today but in the future. What leadership role will those young people take in adapting their musical world to the proliferation of media, to pop culture, to the relationship of serious art or classical music to this new phenomenon in the late twentieth century?

In the United States right after World War Two, the roots of the current educational system were put down. The country's development as a center for musical training, clearly based on European traditions, resulted partly from the country's economic strength at the time and partly from immigration patterns that occurred because of the war. One saw the growth of independent conservatories across the country, all modeled on the nineteenth-century traditions of European training. Something else happened: this system, which traditionally put the primary emphasis on performance, was taken up by music schools and music departments in universities and colleges around the country. A belief grew that performance training of a very, very high level could take place at all institutions. The traditions and expectations that go along with such conservatory training, i.e. the hope that these individuals will find gainful employment through performance, accompanied the system, and can now be found at such universities as the University of Idaho or the University of California, Los Angeles.

In one sense, that's wonderful. One saw in the sixties an enormous growth in the number of students and faculty members seriously engaged in the professional training of musicians. American society at the time, especially college-aged students, was deeply concerned with notions of 'relevancy' and the individual's place in society. Majors such as economics and computer science, certainly business administration, were avoided like the plague. Many students went into English, sociology, political science and music. Statistics show us as many as sixteen to twenty thousand music majors graduated annually, each coming into the field expecting a life in music. Now, even if the quality of education were always at the same high level, which is hardly the case, it would be impossible to employ them all. We realize today that music schools around the country overproduced the number of graduates. Although we're working now to define standards of education in musical performance, it will take many years to rebound from this enormous growth.

We see that we have to encompass the traditions; we hope that we will teach our students to play in tune, to play with other individuals, to have correct rhythm, to have a sense of repertoire and style. At the same time, we hope to instil the adventurousness of spirit that will permit a long life in music. I'm not suggesting that I have a formula for that; the routine of the orchestral musician's life can wear down any person of spirit. We do realize that a twenty-year-old addresses professional life differently than a fifty-year-old. In music, our expectations are lofty. We expect music to enrich us perpetually. We expect to be fully satisfied in our chosen calling. For the fortunate, that is true. For others, that simply won't happen, no matter what training is given, no matter what work context is experienced; it is important that the goals be both lofty and realistic.

The foundation upon which orchestral training and education takes place in the United States is the sincere belief that playing orchestral music is important and needed and enriching. There are teachers who want to produce soloists, and who often speak against the need for orchestral training. But many of those who wish to be soloists, and may in fact be capable of it, will rarely have the opportunity to play Mahler, to play Bruckner, perhaps even to play Wagner; not to experience these composers within the orchestra's context, in concert with other individuals, is to lack a major experience for any musician. Based on that premise, the general educational trend is to have an orchestral requirement within the course of study, whether for a Bachelor's degree or a Master's.

At Juilliard, we have four performing ensembles, two orchestras composed of one hundred students each, that perform the standard repertoire from Bach to Mozart, to Mahler, Stravinsky and Boulez – the works currently performed by professional ensembles. In addition, we have what we call a contemporary ensemble, which is really a smaller orchestra of perhaps sixty players dedicated to playing music of the twentieth century; we hold special festivals, emphasizing the performance of music of the past five to ten years. There is also a chamber orchestra of about forty players which generally specializes in Baroque music. Within that span of ensembles, students are required over a period of four years – two years if they're graduate students – to go to rehearsals for six hours a week. We have seven concerts per ensemble per season, plus each of the ensembles plays one fully staged opera per season. This is not atypical of institutions in the United States, whether the Eastman School or Curtis, which is a smaller institution with one orchestra but still quite active, or Oberlin, or the universities of Illinois, Michigan, Southern California. We have quotas per instrument at Juilliard. We do not admit twenty-five flutes; we have about twelve to sixteen. This is true across the country; we feel that this way the students experience what they need in terms of repertoire. In addition to the rehearsals and performances, we have sectional rehearsals on a regular basis per performance, taken by members of the New York Philharmonic or other members of our faculty. We have repertoire classes for wind instruments which involve playing all of the standard orchestral repertoire in a wind choir, with two pianos supplying the string parts. Percussion are also involved in that. We are just beginning to have orchestral repertoire classes for violin, viola and cello. Violinists and cellists have been reluctant to become involved in orchestral repertoire, a problem that I'll address in a second. Because we feel strongly that chamber music should be an element of the performance program at any school, it is a three-year requirement for strings and for winds, linked closely to the orchestral experience, emphasizing the relationship between playing with two people and playing with twenty.

To address an issue that was brought up peripherally, we also have a liberal arts program for the undergraduates. Twenty-five per cent of the courses taken have to be in subjects other than music. Less than two years ago, we designed a program based on classic literature and the Socratic method. We find that our students respond to it, that they are more knowledgeable of not only their own repertoire but of the world at large. Musicians are used to responding to great works, a score, a string quartet, a piano sonata; they seem to be enthusiastic reading the works of Sartre or Aristotle or Molière as well. We try to relate the courses to the students' roles both as individuals and as artists within society.

The faculty involved with orchestral training consists mostly of the principal players of the New York Philharmonic; other faculty members have been in the Philharmonic or other orchestral settings over the years. We've started a few special projects worth mentioning here. For the past two years, we have had a two-week period of intense interchange with the New York Philharmonic. Last February, for example, we had a joint concert, which was more than just two orchestras on stage; it was ten days of intensive rehearsal with Zubin Mehta and many of the Philharmonic's players. The students' growth was enormous. They not only gained an immense appreciation of what it was to be in an orchestra and understood the production of sound, but the musicians conveyed the respect and sense of pride derived from playing in the orchestra. We had a panel discussion with fifteen members of the orchestra, not just principal players, going on and on about how great it was to play in the Philharmonic, how much they loved the rehearsals and so on. Something beneficial happened in the process. In fact, the students in violin and cello, who were reluctant to become involved in orchestral repertoire, came to me afterwards and requested repertoire classes in their instruments. These are now taking place.

The conflicts raised before do exist, in violin and cello specifically and almost without exception: members of the faculty strongly urge their students to become soloists, telling them that if they are in an orchestra after graduation, they are failures. They don't say it in so many words, but that's the spirit of their communication. This is not only psychologically damaging but a practical error. We are trying to educate the faculty in this case; certainly only one-half of one per cent of musicians will ever have a gainful employment as soloists.

Inviting excellent conductors makes it difficult for the faculty to contend that playing with an orchestra is not a quality experience. This season, we have four concerts in Avery Fisher Hall. We try to bring the best conductors we can to the ensemble and get the musicians to understand how to play in a large hall, to project, to work under very specific circumstances to a compressed schedule of six rehearsals in one week and to perform standard repertoire.

This is a fight, however, that will continue. It is easy to identify a soloist; most are recognized at a very early age, generally between ten and fifteen for the violin, piano and cello; even those soloists are required to be in our orchestra. But that does not mean that they will not be chamber musicians, that they will not be soloists eventually. It's impossible, and pretentious, for us to chart the course of human events. But it is important that we give our students as great a breadth of exposure as possible. Wind players and percussion players see their ultimate goal as being in an orchestra; string players for the most part envision themselves first as soloists, second as chamber musicians and last as orchestral players – with, perhaps, teaching squeezed in somewhere.

Finally, the financial realities of the musical marketplace take me to what I reluctantly refer to as the art of the audition. In conferences that I've attended, the point raised here is always made: conservatories don't train the students adequately to take an audition and to perform in an orchestra over a long period of time. But there is always a successful applicant, and the musician hired is rarely let go after the ten-year period comes to an end. Generally, he or she is sufficiently integrated to be successful. At an audition, the candidate is expected to play everything perfectly, to produce immediately the type of sound and the camaraderie and sense of human spirit looked for by that ensemble. That is eventually achieved, but after a three or four month break-in period.

Before we look at conservatories as the breeding ground of malcontent, we should look at the broader fact: we are working with young people who have many options ahead of them. We hope they will have enough education, and sense of human spirit, and love for their art – which is the essential point – to be happy and flourish in any context, as soloist, chamber musician, orchestral player, administrator or teacher.

GORDON GETTY: Mr Polisi, you said that about sixteen to twenty thousand students graduate every year from a reputable conservatory or major in music from university. Can you estimate how many of those go on to musical careers?

JOSEPH POLISI: We don't have solid statistics; although I know a few specific institutions, they really don't tell the whole story. Of the Juilliard students, it seems about seventy per cent are primarily employed making music or dance and drama.

ERNEST FLEISCHMANN: Among the many positive aspects of Juilliard's approach to preparing musicians for orchestral careers, one major problem remains. The school has a good relationship with the New York Philharmonic; it's exciting for students to work in that very high-caliber professional atmosphere. But there are nearly fifteen hundred orchestras in the United States, and in Europe there are hundreds of small provincial orchestras. The positions in those orchestras, I'm afraid, still entail the sort of drudgery, the frustrating mind- and art-numbing existence that we're all afraid of. We need to address ourselves to the improvement of those situations. A lot depends on a) the training of better-equipped, less career-oriented, more music-oriented conductors, and b) on the expectations of managements and audiences in those secondary and tertiary situations.

I disagree with Mr Polisi's statement that a vacancy in a major orchestra can always be filled. After five different lots of auditions this last year in Los Angeles, for each of which we had upward of two hundred applications, only two positions were filled. For three other positions we were unable to find musicians of sufficiently high caliber. Maybe later there will be a chance to talk more about this; I would be interested in Mr Polisi's opinion of the pre-professional training beyond the conservatory that goes on in summer schools like Tanglewood or the Los Angeles Philharmonic Institute, on the cusp, as it were, of the profession.

KARSTEN WITT: Mr Polisi, you are in a very special situation: at Juilliard and the other schools you mentioned there is a very high standard for the students. Therefore you are able to have homogeneous groups in orchestras – which is not true for every conservatory. For example, in Germany we have sixteen *Musikhochschulen*; most of them have certain good classes and others which are weaker. In this situation it is very difficult to build up an orchestra within a school which can effectively prepare people for the profession. The technique of orchestral playing is not however education's most important task. We have academies, for example, at some professional German orchestras, which can slowly introduce young musicians to orchestral playing by participation in rehearsals.

In America you have an advantage compared to our German institutions, in that the music school is not only a training place but a cultural institution. Contemporary music, for example, is performed. The students, playing seriously in different ensembles, not only work with their teachers in closed classes but take part in public culture, in that the conservatory is itself already public. The university in America, as far as I understand, is often the most important cultural center. In Europe, the theater or concert hall is the center; conservatories regard themselves only as training places.

PIERRE BOULEZ: I would like to ask a question, wearing my composer's hat this time: is there a constant educational relationship between composers and orchestras? Whatever I learned about the orchestra, I learned conducting. There was absolutely no relationship between performance and a composer teaching composition classes. Something done in this direction would be really path-breaking.

JOSEPH POLISI: Generally the orchestral players want to experience the standard repertoire, so that they will audition well. We've carefully structured the experience over an entire year, so that student composers have an opportunity to hear their music in an orchestral setting. It's very easy to perform the composers' chamber works, which we do all the time, but to do a full orchestral reading or performance is another story. We've done two things. For graduating students, or students who have written a work considered worthy by the composition faculty – by the way, we have about twenty-five composition students – we have a three-hour reading and recording of the work. The rehearsal, of an hour and a half to two hours, is recorded as well. It isn't ideal: the works are worthy of more rehearsal, but for those students who don't get a fully fledged performance, it's at least useful.

We've also instituted a competition for composition students. Each year two scores are chosen to be performed at the next season's concerts, alongside whatever else is being performed. At least two composers get full, public, orchestral performances each season. At the moment, we find it adequate; half of the composers are in a formative stage, working and eager to have their music performed, but not quite ready in terms of skills and craft to have it done.

PIERRE BOULEZ: I was speaking about analysis of existing works. For instance, if you have an analysis class on the *Rite of Spring*, the orchestra plays excerpts and instrumental combinations, to see how they are superimposed. In some places you need to hear how it sounds, and after that to hear the rest of the orchestra. With a work like *Erwartung*, unless you have actually heard it, you don't know the work. For students of composition, it's essential with such a piece to have a three-hour session with the composition teacher and orchestra. Can you provide that?

JOSEPH POLISI: No. When we did the *Rite of Spring* with Zubin Mehta, the composition students were present at all rehearsals with their scores. They did not choose what parts were analyzed; Zubin did. It was a fantastic experience however. You're right though, we don't have a hundred-piece orchestra available to the composers to that extent.

PETER PASTREICH: Mr Fleischmann commented on the deadening life in smaller orchestras: having worked in a number of them, I would say that generalization should not be made. Some very exciting things are going on in some quite medium-to-smaller-sized cities in the United States.

On the difficulty of finding good people at audition: I'm increasingly convinced that the real issue has little to do with conservatory graduates. It concerns good musicians, already employed, unwilling to submit themselves to the humiliation and frustrations of a very ineffective hiring system. That we're not getting good applicants doesn't prove there aren't good players out there.

Finally, Mr Polisi said that twenty-five per cent of the conservatory courses are in the liberal arts. I have a feeling, which my experience seems to reinforce, but which I'd like to see proved wrong, that students spend the least time on that one course in four. You can't compare a great books course, where they read six great books a year, with four courses in violin or in harmony for which they practice and study day and night. Orchestral musicians pay a heavy price for their lack of broad education when they're out in life and in orchestras.

JOSEPH POLISI: The basis of a conservatory education is education in the performing arts, and in an individual, specific discipline. The freshmen we see are highly motivated as musicians; that's a choice they've made. In a liberal arts situation, a profession is rarely chosen the first year. The motivational structure is very different, not right or wrong, simply different. We have instituted an intensive, integrated experience; the quality of the classroom teaching and of the discussion and material studied compares with their orchestral rehearsals, their theory classes, their chamber music coachings. The students no longer decide on the order of priorities. If we do Goethe's *Faust*, it's not in relation to Gounod but to the concept of the artist as hero. Parenthetically, the students decided, in response to their study of Goethe, that the image most beneficial to them was the artist as pauper; they articulated a belief that opposed financial benefit to art. We try to help them see that this is also the wrong image to pursue. We can't duplicate a four-year liberal arts college education, but I think that what we're doing is substantive.

ISAAC STERN: There is a difference between the expectations and realizations of young musicians in the United States and those in Europe – in this case, a quantitative one. So many large orchestras pay very high salaries to newcomers, the idea of having to be poor to join an orchestra no longer exists in the United States. It's one of the problems; many young people, straight out of school, totally unprepared, immediately begin with an annual salary of thirty-five to forty thousand dollars, which is unheard of for a beginning orchestral player in Europe.

Many of you have touched on the quality of teachers. Where are the teachers who can awaken the bright youngster's natural potential curiosity, spark that ignition, help them examine the music correctly and with some enthusiasm? The people entrusted with these young minds and talents are not really properly trained. All too often, the music 'educator' in the United States is neither educated nor musical, but simply has what *passes* for a degree at some obscure college. Quality and how to achieve it: that's something for us to think about.

I would like to ask Anna Lindal to read her paper on the question of young people in connection with their playing in orchestras.

Young Musicians: Training & Tradition

ANNA LINDAL: I have been involved with various orchestras for about seven years, the last three as assistant concertmaster in the Stockholm Philharmonic. That's a fairly short time to get a proper overview of the complex activities of an orchestra, but it may be enough to be able to express and hold a number of new points of view. Let's begin with the question of training. I have spoken about this with many young musicians, and I myself remember what it was like to join an orchestra as a novice. Although you're highly qualified as an instrumentalist and although you bring a lot of enthusiasm with you, the initial period is fairly difficult. It is exciting, but also stressful; stimulating, but also inhibiting. Adapting to the collective is a process that involves both pleasure and constraint. This is true not just of playing but of all the various laws which obtain in any orchestra.

Often the training you receive is of little help when it comes to playing in an orchestra. The orchestras at music colleges generally fail to encourage any responsible orchestral work. They rarely rehearse within a fixed period or with a fixed aim, and virtually never enable the students, for example, to work with professional orchestral musicians. Of course, this varies according to the country and the college concerned, but it's often the case that players train to become orchestral musicians within the orchestra itself. That's why most orchestras really ought to take more interest in establishing their own orchestral schools in order to ensure continuity and quality within the profession.

But we don't just need continuity in this profession, we also need change, a more dynamic approach and new ideas. You might expect the younger generation to bring these qualities with them as a matter of course, but that's not always the case. If you look at the sort of training we receive, you can perhaps understand why. You'd have to look a long way to find a form of professional training more conservative than ours. We're generally trained in a tradition which, at best, belonged to the previous generation. You only have to compare it with other forms of professional training to realize that we are unique in this respect. Just imagine what it would be like if doctors enjoyed the same sort of training as we musicians. Not many people would be grateful for that kind of medical treatment. All right, our responsibility is different; it is a musical responsibility, but that doesn't mean that it should be under-valued.

What I object to about our present training can be summed up in three points. First, *what* we play. In instrumental teaching, virtually no contemporary music is played. We do not get to know this music, and certainly do not get to understand it. We scarcely ever master the special playing techniques and new ways of writing. Even before we begin our professional activity, we have been overtaken.

Secondly, *how* we play. All the interpretational innovations in the so-called classical repertoire, such as the revolution which our conception of Baroque and Classical music has undergone during the last fifteen to twenty years, scarcely gain a foothold in music colleges until they are firmly fixed in the musical life of the country.

Thirdly, *who* are we playing for? New kinds of concerts are rarely, if ever, discussed at music colleges. These three points are then automatically carried over into the orchestra. Of course, there is a certain interaction, but you could also describe it as a vicious circle. The orchestras demand musicians who are trained in the 'traditional' way, nothing more, and so the colleges train such musicians. And vice versa: the colleges train musicians who have few opportunities to change conditions in musical life. In the orchestra itself, there is accordingly no further training, except on the individual level. The new things with which we ought to be confronted fail to materialize, with the exception of the few modern works which we do actually perform – always with too little rehearsal time and often with mediocre and uninspired performances as a result. It would be a good idea, for example, to organize seminars with composers in order to reduce the mutual distrust and to replace it with a degree of understanding. Especially when commissioned works are to be performed, groups could be formed out of the orchestra to work together with the composer.

As far as forms of concerts and our contact with the public are concerned, I find a kind of vicious circle here too. *We* are afraid to change, in case we drive away our sacrosanct subscription audiences; the audiences get used to hearing more or less the same works all the time, and come to resist all change. Music institutions concern themselves more and more with the audience they already have, but very little, if at all, with the people who never go to concerts. To waken these people's wishes and curiosity might not be easy, but it is a challenge, perhaps the most important challenge to confront us. With a little imagination, you can do a lot. The possibilities are enormous, including advance introductions to concerts, concerts with commentaries, concerts which go out to find their audience, free concerts and, most importantly, good school concerts. There's an infinite amount that can be done, and it doesn't have to cost a lot – at all events it represents a gain in the long term.

Series of concerts with special themes like contemporary music are generally completely useless. What I mean is that we offer the audience what they already know and expect, and therefore we do not expose a single new ear to this kind of music. Programs should be as mixed as possible; it's the unusual combinations and unexpected connections which turn an audience of passive listeners into one of active participants.

I'd like to give a new job to our friends in the press. Instead of providing smug little reports after each concert, describing our work as 'successful' or 'not', and generally putting the readers off the music, why can't they write introductory pieces in advance, describing the various works, composers, different periods, etc. This would make more positive use of their critical competence.

How is the heavy, inflexible, conservative or, to put it crudely, boring orchestra to be transformed into a living, dynamic and creative musical institution? Things do look bad at present. Institutions, worried about their subsidies, play it safe. They don't try anything new. It's a bit like the ostrich hiding its head in the sand, and it's just as effective. The opposite is the only possible solution: at a time of entrenchment and economic threat, we should be looking for new solutions, finding new ideas and carrying them out. Otherwise we'll stagnate.

For my own part, I imagine the orchestra of the future as something quite different – rather like a music bank, for want of a better word, with several subsections, each specializing in a particular area, such as modern music, performance on old instruments, string and wind ensembles, chamber orchestras. The advantages would be enormous. Greater flexibility in all areas: program planning, types of concerts, division of labor; greater responsibility for each musician, and hence, more pleasure in his or her work. I leave others to work out the details of such an institution, but new perspectives would open if these ideas could be developed further.

That music is necessary, yesterday as much as in the future, needn't be argued, but we can't rely only on its momentum. Music is an expression of its time. We must address ourselves to the time in which we live. Our own age is, amongst other things, the age of mass media; people are more and more becoming passive consumers of every kind of visual and aural product, good, bad and indifferent. But it is a chance for us, with our live music, to exert a provocative influence by seeking people out and activating them.

MICHAL SMOIRA-COHN: I was asked to prepare a paper on educating an orchestra. I did so, but I will not read it. Many important problems have been raised. The situation at Juilliard seems to be paradise on earth, but life is not like that. Our music world is a very difficult world. A youngster, having decided to study the violin – and let us not forget that the strings are still the bulk of the orchestra – studies against contemporary social norms. I know violin students who put their violins in guitar cases when they go along the street to their classes, so that their friends will not mock them. The student does all this because he really wants to achieve something. He wants, in ten years time, to stand on the stage and not only get all the limelight and everything that goes with it – why shouldn't he want it? – but also make his music. And then he sits somewhere in the tenth seat in the orchestra. As Isaac said, in the past to belong to a great orchestra was something to be proud of. It's not so anymore. It's true that in the United States you earn a great deal of money playing in an orchestra, but it's not so in other countries.

Now, you will agree with me that today we cannot talk of 'music.' We have to talk about 'musics,' there are so many different kinds: the Baroque concerto, played once again on the original instruments, and the piece of music written the day before yesterday, with its quite different demands. These are different arts. Sometimes when I think about the music of today, I see before me an animal with a hundred legs, legs that go very quickly. Each leg is moving in a different direction, somehow without considering the other legs, and the animal's heart breaks, literally, because every leg is moving in a different direction. You cannot make those things come together.

Miss Lindal spoke of the music critic's failure; as I myself for a time was a music critic, I take the blame. I agree one hundred per cent with what she says. We are all moving on our separate roads. Should we all be free to do exactly what pleases us? I'm not sure anymore. I'm not sure that it shouldn't be like ancient times, when a bishop or kaiser or prince decided what music was going to be written and what played, what the people were going to hear. I'm not sure that this was so very wrong – we got out of it such a wonderful musical repertoire that we can't get rid of it. That is our problem: we cannot get rid of Mozart and Beethoven. We don't dress like that anymore. We don't live in those houses anymore. But their music is still with us. It still serves us. It's an excellent kind of music but we are fed up with it, because it is so different from the excellent things being done today. The public however is not interested and is not ready to go into the twentieth century.

The people making the music policies of the Western world should put their heads together and see how all those different legs can be made to move in unison.

RICHARD BAECHI: I found myself in extraordinary sympathy with Miss Lindal's paper. As I was able to read her paper in advance, and study some of her ideas in detail, I should like to ask her a couple of questions. As an orchestral manager, but also as a concert organizer in the Tonhalle in Zurich, where we organize well over a hundred concerts per season, I find myself reproached for sticking my head in the sand and not being prepared to slaughter the sacred cow, the subscription audience, and for not having enough imagination not only to plan new types of concerts but to realize those plans. Every year, when we plan the season's program, we discuss this question of the willingness to innovate. We want to realize new ways to communicate music, new kinds of concerts – and time and again our wings are cut by the orchestra's financial basis, which underlies its very existence. If we were to put your ideas into practice, you might find yourself without a job, losing with it your livelihood.

Two examples of the realities of concert programming will suffice. During the festival, we tried to have an evening of Lutoslawski with leading interpreters, Heinz Holliger and his wife. We performed his Third Symphony, a very important work, and two other pieces – and we ran up an enormous deficit. We tried performing Schnittke's Fourth Violin Concerto with Kremer, in the form you suggest, a mixed program, and again there was a huge loss. We are happy to accept these deficits, and we try to absorb them, but there's a limit to what we can do.

You're clearly aware that today's symphony orchestra has to function at a time of threat, in a threatening environment. I'd be grateful if we could develop your ideas further, perhaps taking as our starting point your suggestion for a music bank: it would help to bring your ideas, your vision one might call it, closer to the actuality. Nonetheless, I'd like to thank you very much for your honest and interesting suggestions.

PIERRE VOZLINSKY: Mr Baechi, was this Lutoslawski concert completely isolated in its preparation? Did it just come out of the blue and disappear back into the blue?

RICHARD BAECHI: It took place within the framework of the month-long festival program. In Lutoslawski we found not only a composer but a conductor; we arranged an introductory event with him. In other words, preparation and information played a role. And this was in a city where Hans Rosbaud was active over a long period, where audiences ought to be versed in this kind of music and accept such concerts unprotestingly, even if they involve an element of provocation.

JOSEPH TAL: The whole problem is not a musical problem, not one of composers or musicians, but of education. Because no educator has given thought to it, we are unprepared. We continue with public educational programs geared to the past, not to the future. They were very good programs, and they achieved tremendous results, but times have changed.

In the conservatory, we learn to play an instrument; that doesn't mean we learn to listen to a work. Very, very few teachers are able to direct students to want to listen. They imitate the teacher instead. How to listen is a subject of education. To whom does a musician speak? To the public, and we have no common language when we speak to an untrained public, other than uncontrollable feelings based on all kinds of past conditions. To my mind, this is the most important point. Thankful for our fine analysis of today's problems, I am curious to know what tomorrow will be like.

BASIL TSCHAIKOV: Large numbers of people, having had an opportunity to learn an instrument in school, find playing very agreeable and enjoyable. Playing in a youth orchestra is a tremendous experience; a few decide they would like to go on doing it. But there is a great difference between earning your living by playing a musical instrument and being a musician. We're dedicated to the notion that we should prepare people to serve the composer and the audience, to be musicians making music with other people, not serve themselves as either amateurs or 'professionals' – that is, relate their success to how good a position they have in the orchestra or how much money they earn or how many sessions they do. All of us must know promising musicians who, by the time they were in their middle or late twenties, have to all intents and purposes died as musicians. When they go into an orchestra, that should be the start of their growth as musicians. Learning how to lead one minute and to follow the next. One moment to know just what the conductor wants and the next moment to be inspirational, in response to the music and to the audience and to their colleagues in the orchestra. We need the inspiration of each other; I have heard concerts where one player has, by the way he played a particular solo, raised the entire level of the program.

When you're a professional musician, you have to play when you don't feel like it. You have to play music you love in ways you don't like. You have to play music you don't like with the same intensity and integrity that you do music which you love. You have to sit next to people you don't like. Someone who's always a semiquaver ahead of you, or a little bit flatter than you. You have to learn to serve this extraordinary activity, this incredible organism, which is, I think, a jewel in the crown of civilization, a microcosm of society at its best: the orchestra. Even after all these many years of being associated with an orchestra, I still believe it capable of giving the greatest joy.

If I may finish on a very high-flown note: it is my belief – and I've been lucky enough in my life to work with most of the great conductors over the last few decades – that you cannot have a great performance without a conductor who can make a group of a hundred people play as if they were one. When that happens, you are like an eagle flying over Everest. The trouble with being an eagle is that sometimes you only fly over Mont Blanc, occasionally over small hills and sometimes in the valleys. And the higher you've been, the deeper the valleys seem. This is the problem that people who play for a living every day, every week, have to come to terms with. All of us have the intention of serving the audience; that's the reason we are musicians, that people out there want to hear those noises. It enriches their lives. If it doesn't do that then there's no point in us being managers or having orchestras or being players. If we're dedicated to that, we should be dedicated to creating the circumstances in which young musicians, starting out on this road, do so with the right aspirations: not just to earn their living successfully or otherwise as players but to dedicate themselves to this noble task.

GEORGE WEIDENFELD: The question of the status of the performing artist in a consumer society is fundamental. Can we not, without resorting to state patronage or to the trappings of controlled art, address ourselves to the question of how to enhance the musician's status and therefore self-respect? I have a successful model in my mind: Sir John Reith's BBC was a public corporation, yet it was not part of the state apparatus. My very first job, when I arrived in England, was at a BBC establishment in the West Country. Arriving at the end of the night shift, I would see that élite corps, the BBC engineers, arriving in their tweed jackets and flannel trousers. They thought and felt that they were the lords of the universe, and were, because Sir John Reith told them they were. They had equal status with the program division. They were considered very important people, proud of what they were doing in a society in which the engineer was in general held in very low esteem.

Society, particularly our consumer society with its gargantuan income differential, must address the status of those who work in the performing arts. This is part of the problem of education, and something which we must consider.

ISAAC STERN: In this room, in this studio, we've been working for some years with young talents. This country is blessed with a quota of talent far out of proportion to its size, and I've been part of an organization involved with most of the scholarships given to young people in this country – and I mean young, between the ages of about seven and seventeen. In a country of this size it doesn't make much sense to have four hundred pianists, one viola player and, every three years, one trombone player. It has been necessary to take a good hard look at the scholarship program's operation.

But there was another problem: those gifted ones returned time and time again, because there was a lack of musical direction given to the study of the instrument. The student was taught how to play, but never why to play. So we began the string unit, concerned principally with chamber music; in the last two or three years, it has been quite astonishing to hear these kids play Mozart or Prokofiev quartets, or whatever the case may be. Little kids, eleven, twelve, thirteen years old, play with understanding, with love, with attention. Their teachers have a real desire to lead them in the right direction. All of these things began, admittedly in a small environment, because some attention was paid. Lately we have undertaken, with a leading composer, a three-year planned program of training in ancillary musical studies – the history of musical performance, counterpoint theory. We are really using the group of kids now enrolled as a pilot program, to show other institutions how they might reorganize their teaching standards.

The last thing that we have embarked on, which I submit as a basis for discussion, is a program which I have seen working in Hungary, one of the great training programs for nonprofessional, musically interested people. Many of you will know about Zoltán Kodály's method, which uses no instruments but the human voice. I was first impressed when I saw his classes in Budapest some fifteen years ago or more, of various grades of pupils, from age six to eighteen, pursuing general studies. The secret is highly trained teachers, using hand signals to indicate melody: to see a class of six-, seven-, eight-year-old children take a melody by dictation, by hand signals, to listen to the teacher telling a non-music class, 'Give me a Haydn cadence, a Bach cadence and a Mozart cadence!'

and hear the children do it! Children not trained in music got close to understanding differences of style; they had an idea of musical sound in their ears, using melodies familiar to them from the folk songs of their country. The end result, by the time they were eighteen, was young children singing *a cappella* more beautifully than you hear the most professional chorus singing. And not one of them is involved in training for music as a profession. This is simply the best kind of audience preparation you can imagine.

We are trying to do that here. Some people are going to Hungary for a year's training and then coming back to get materials and to try it in two experimental schools. It's a long-range investment. It takes time. It takes care. It takes dedicated people, and it takes great patience to wait for the results, but I feel it's a major demonstration of what might be done in education, so that we have an interested, aware and educated listener at the other end.

JOSEPH POLISI: Miss Lindal's very provocative and important statement presented a bleak landscape in relation to education. Did you, when you gave your paper in Stockholm, have a chance to speak with education officials about your concern, and if so, was there any effort to effect some of those ideas – or were they rejected out of hand as being perhaps too radical? What was the reaction?

ANNA LINDAL: Nothing. I think the invitation to this conference is the first reaction I've had to the speech at all.

HANS LANDESMANN: So far in this discussion, we have been generalizing in terms of the Anglo-Saxon world; perhaps some of our comments will not apply to the continent, or to Eastern European countries, where there is also a very important musical life. In Eastern Europe, although the general education is not of a higher standard than it is in the West, the public's curiosity for contemporary music is absolutely tremendous. They don't need any lectures or other devices to bring them into the auditorium. Contemporary concerts, whether in Budapest or Russia or Prague, are very, very well attended; there's an innate curiosity about what is going on in the world.

The position of the musicians is very different from that of most continental countries. As either state or city employees, most of the players have a different outlook in terms of security: they are absolutely secure up to the time they retire. After that, they get a pension. They don't have to fear losing their jobs and becoming paupers. The same thing applies to the orchestras, funded by the state, or by the city, or by a radio station, which again is always state owned. Our Western system has gone down a lot. For many institutions, whose finances are extremely well grounded – I might mention the Vienna State Opera or the Salzburg Festival – the funds have prevented people from thinking, from being imaginative. At least in our country, those institutions which have to look for money and develop schemes are the ones who bring life into the musical world. I don't think we should look at strong funding as the basis of a good music program.

ISAAC STERN: Mr Landesmann, would you say that in the Eastern European countries with which you are familiar, those residents who are not constantly inundated by the enormous number of distractions available to the residents of Western Europe and the United States, by way of television, movies, theatre, are more curious and more susceptible to those things that pique their curiosity? Is there any relationship in your mind?

HANS LANDESMANN: There's a definite relationship. In addition, as you know, some contemporary music was forbidden for a long time, which must play a role as well. Forbidden fruit attracts the greatest interest. But really, it's the kind of atmosphere in these countries that makes the audience more curious.

FRANZ XAVER OHNESORG: Looking at this marvelous circle, I wonder: shouldn't we take the opportunity to discuss the education of the orchestra's directors, as well as that of the audience and musicians? The right method of leading a symphony orchestra; the right management philosophy; how to find a way between hierarchy and the democratic philosophy that seeks the orchestra's opinion in making programs and deciding what the orchestra as a whole should do. It is really a question of the musicians' motivation and of leading them to find this right way to run the orchestra. Should the structure include a chief conductor and a general manager, or should we have a so-called general director who is a sort of artistic director? The German structure relies on a general music director – who hardly speaks with God, much less with musicians. The musicians should know that they are members of this company, the symphony orchestra, which is indeed the crown of civilization. The right corporate identity is also important, both for the orchestra itself and for the audience; its development is a creative task, if one plans to find the right environment for the orchestra and for bringing audiences to the symphony. Most orchestras in Germany are run by an administrator, who could just as easily run a factory or public services, but if fundraising is a necessary part of the structure, one does marketing. We have Harvard Business School and we have Fontainebleu, where you can learn to run a factory, but we don't have a school where directors can learn to run a symphony orchestra. If you look at directors' biographies, it's evident that each spends a great deal of life learning music and a large part learning management; it may fit together, but there's no accepted system of education.

SEMYON BYCHKOV: We talk about the musicians' feelings and the composers' – all of that is very much affected by those who are supposed to lead orchestral institutions, that is, the conductors. Without the vision, one doesn't have the necessary musical and human qualities. Then everyone is in trouble.

That the word 'career' has become an obsession, particularly among conductors, concerns me a great deal. Great orchestras operate, especially in the Anglo-Saxon world, extremely efficiently. Which means very little rehearsal time, tremendous speed in learning the right notes – and then the concert. If there isn't a disaster, if the person is technically efficient, he or she gains a reputation for reliability and speed, and a great career begins. If by accident the person finds him or herself with an orchestra of conservatory level, or with a provincial orchestra that doesn't qualify as one of the great artistic institutions of the world, suddenly this person is unable to make them sound any better than they did a week before. There is no foundation, no inside knowledge of the orchestra. That cannot be acquired overnight and cannot be speeded up. Every person has a specific pace of development, a length of time required to think about the music and to practice it.

Conducting is different from any other performing profession; a pianist, a vocalist, an instrumentalist has the opportunity to work with the instrument. A conductor does not. A conductor needs an orchestra in order to develop experience and to develop ideas. On the other hand, I was brought up to hold the ethical view that in order to have a right to stand in front of an orchestra, one has to have something to say that would be of interest and of help to those one is supposed to lead.

It's a Catch 22 situation – and that's where not only the lack of a system but the lack of conducting schooling is so evident. A certain period, indispensable to one's artistic development and human development as well, is skipped. With enough talent, human and musical, one operates immediately on a certain professional level, which is not really warranted. Later on the holes in the background become evident to everyone. The present is built on the past; the future won't exist without a present.

One learns a great deal by observing the lives of great artists. Great conductors invariably – it doesn't matter if one admires Mr Karajan or if one's favorite is Furtwängler – have something in common. They had years of study. There is really no substitute for that. But in the last two generations, this has changed. Now we have over thirty so-called major orchestras in America, major not only in terms of the budget but also in quality of playing. For five years we've had many original symphonies. And very often orchestras reach a pinnacle of musical maturity, a level higher than that of the people who are supposed to lead them. This in turn will breed frustration and resentment on the part of the members of an orchestra. It's hard enough to be controlled by someone standing on the podium; it is even harder if you feel that the person knows less than you do.

For almost five years before coming to the West, I studied at the Leningrad Conservatory where there is a tremendous, well-considered tradition of teaching conducting. Rimsky-Korsakov called conducting, if I can translate it literally, a dark business, a dark horse. He was right. It was dark to him and is still dark to many of us; much of it is unknown, a lot of it is quite mystical. But one needs to know many things that can be taught. What makes people think that just because one is a very good musician, one can stand up and be an equally terrific conductor? Conducting must be studied, it needs to be thought about and developed. This is something missing right now; some of the great teachers, like Swarowsky in Vienna, are no longer with us, and I don't see new teachers who continue their tradition.

PIERRE BOULEZ: There is certainly a lack of conducting expertise, although I'm not really the man to speak about that since I myself studied conducting from nature, let us say. If one really believed in education, then every good performer should have very good students, which is definitely not true. You have very good students who come from very bad teachers, and vice versa. Education is, in part, a great game of chance. You can't foresee everything; as with genetics, good results can come from bad beginnings.

We spoke about the taste of musicians, the conservatism of audiences, the conservatism of some musicians – but let's speak about the taste of conductors and performers. For a couple of years, I was in a position to discuss programs; the managers present here will not contradict me when I say it is very difficult to get an original program from conductors. If you propose Mahler's First, they propose Mahler's Ninth; when you say that has already been performed three times, they propose Four; you say it was performed seven times, and they are completely out of ideas. The repertoire is sometimes very small, because you have this mill. Some people, specialized in their repertoire, study all season; you cannot get anything out of them but the four or five pieces they are conducting that season. This makes it very difficult to have original ideas. In a museum, you can see Rembrandt's *Night Watch*, a very important picture. But you also see paintings by dozens of other, lesser artists. It's interesting to see why Rembrandt is a genius. In the world of music, we present only the best work, divorced from the historical element. It's as much the wrong idea to present only masterpieces as it is to bring out everything that you can find in a library. Programming ideas is the business of the managers and musical directors. As long as I was a musical director, I thought of making programs a little more interesting. The blame does not rest only on education, only on the orchestral musicians, only on institutions. At the core of the problem, we must ask, What is the imagination of conductors and performers?

ERNEST FLEISCHMANN: It's now twenty years since I wrote an article for *High Fidelity* entitled 'Who Runs our Orchestras and Who Should?' It dealt with the development of the jet-set conductor, travelling around the world with luggage in hand – which doesn't have to be checked, because it only contains five or six programs. There are enough orchestras prepared to buy those five or six programs. By doing them often, the conductors come to know them very well. The trouble is, there's a shortage of music directors, and those very conductors, with their five or six programs a year, are also expected to become musical directors.

I pleaded at that time for a change in the system. I compared boards of directors in England and in the United States. In England, the orchestras are run by musicians, who are working tremendously hard. They must of course concentrate on their playing and so don't have the opportunity to acquire the know-how and the ability to make both programs and policy. Programs are part of artistic policy.

In the United States, where boards of directors consist of corporate heads and specialists from all kinds of fields – except that of running an artistic institution – the situation is similar. I pleaded then for the creation of supermanagers, those who can cope with the tremendous problems of structure, finance, unions and so on, but who can also help music directors develop programming and develop all those things they have to take care of when the conductor isn't there – which is at least half the year. How do we educate those managers? I had a conversation with one of Mr Bychkov's younger colleagues earlier this week, who said, 'I'm tired of being jet set because jet set causes jet lag, and it's time I put music before career.'

If only more younger conductors can be persuaded by us older folk to think along those lines!

In a way, we're preaching to the converted here. We need to start preaching to the masses of the unconverted. We all have colleagues, whether musicians, managers or politicians, who influence what we do. They need to hear from us about these things. Managers, particularly in those areas where business schools turn out arts managers, need to do everything possible to equip themselves with a great deal more knowledge of the actual art form. It's our job as much as anyone else's to keep up with what's going on in music, to keep our minds open, to exercise those leadership roles for which we're really appointed. Managers so often say their boards restrict them – it's up to us to educate our boards. When one speaks to board members one to one, they listen; they're not stupid people. Most of them are on a board because they really do care.

PETER HEYWORTH: I was amused to hear Pierre Boulez espouse education for everybody except conductors. I'm sure he's absolutely right. I can't for a moment believe that conductors can be educated. They learn: in the past they took small jobs, and if they got good, they took better ones and they worked their way up in a sort of hierarchy. Now God knows how they get jobs or what persuades the managers to engage them in some cases. They may be very good television performers. They may have very good agents. Anyway, they're around and available because of aircraft. I suspect – and hope that I'm right – we're getting to the end of a very bad period of conducting.

When I started as a critic thirty years ago, conducting was generally on a much higher and more serious level. There were many old-fashioned figures who had worked their way up slowly and had time to learn their jobs properly before they reached the top. In the last twenty or thirty years, for many reasons, there's been a sort of débâcle. The recording companies, pirouetting conductors to the top, seize on a figure; they put the screws on the orchestras or vice versa. God knows how it's all done, but the concerts one goes to are not always as satisfying as they once were. But I sense among young conductors – this probably applies to soloists too – a general awareness that this is really no way of running one's life and no way of dedicating oneself to a musical career.

Mr Bertini said something to me about not wanting to be constantly airborne from one place to another. Perhaps the time is coming when conductors will be willing to take a job and do it in one place and reserve a very limited amount of their time for travel – more as it used to be.

CHRISTOPHER BISHOP: I would just like to correct Mr Flei-schmann in a slight mistake, which he wouldn't have made twenty years ago. There are other orchestras in England than the four independent London orchestras. The London orches-tras are self-governing and the players run their own affairs, but most of the other orchestras in England are perfectly normal and they are contracted. This second group includes those of the BBC.

I should like to propose, from my bishop-type seat, an edict that, in future, one of the best things we could possibly do in this jet age would be to insist that no conductor be allowed to hold more than one musical directorship. At present, if any conductor holds two, he automatically goes and works for the one that produces the best money. I won't cite examples, but this has happened often recently. It's one thing if the two places are close to each other, but if one is one side of the Atlantic and one's the other, anyone who's tried to fix programs with a jet-lagged conductor will know what problems are involved.

It's an incredible shame and outrage that this should be the case. If Mr X was not allowed to be music director of two orchestras, then another person would be able to direct one of them, and there would be more conductors around. The paucity of conductors is absolutely horrifying.

PIERRE BOULEZ: May I defend myself, because I was in this situation a few years ago. I did not find it difficult. Orchestras no longer accept the idea of being conducted by one person for the entire season, as was done before World War Two. I've seen even George Szell during his time in Cleveland conduct almost seventy per cent of the concerts. But now the season grows longer and longer: you have to delegate approximately half the season to guests. The idea of principal guest conductor, one person present for more concerts than another one may be, is a kind of security for the rest of the season. But if you concentrate on two orchestras, as I have done, it is possible to devote equal time to each, spending great blocks of time while you are there and, when they are fed up with you, going on to another place.

CHRISTOPHER BISHOP: For the young conductor, if you hold only one job and take off four or five months, you have an opportunity to study those scores that you may need in the future when you may be forced to hold two jobs.

PETER HEYWORTH: If I may reply to Pierre Boulez. When Szell was conducting seventy per cent of the Cleveland Orchestra's concerts, he was conducting an orchestra of an enormously high standard.

PIERRE BOULEZ: Yes, I agree, but that seventy per cent was probably only twelve weeks. That's what I meant to express. When he was sure his orchestra was in good shape and had reached that high level, he conducted in Europe. He was not just tied to the Cleveland Orchestra. I was invited to conduct in Germany while I was with the BBC, but refused. If I am working with an orchestra, I would rather do tours with that orchestra than go from one to another. I think that's the right policy.

KARSTEN WITT: On the crisis of conductors and the lack of good and permanent conductors: I'm convinced this is linked to the crisis of the orchestral community which we discussed before. The role of the conductor nowadays is one which very few people can take over. First of all, the musicians will accept very few people in this role. The provincial orchestras have as good an idea of what a good conductor has to know and has to be like as any other better orchestra, although, as they make careers for themselves in their own regions, they really give the conductor a chance to develop. The real reason that so many conductors jet around all the time is that they don't dare to stay in one place and keep doing different things, one after another.

The relationship may be one of cooperation between conductor and orchestra, at least in orchestras when there are few rehearsals and the two are really dependent on each other. In Germany, where you spend a week, or even two, in Baden-Baden to work on one program, the musicians know everything about the person standing in front of them – and there are very, very few people who survive in this situation. One hundred people, who know very well what they are doing, are waiting for the mistake to be made. Only if the musicians themselves are responsible for the result, and also responsible for the conductor, whom they have themselves invited, may you come to a cooperative relationship. When you have to work with who's there, it may become easier.

This structure would be helpful as well in another area we've been considering: programming. If you discuss programs with musicians you will get different ideas, which won't surface in a discussion between conductor and manager. Just before I left for Jerusalem, Henze – two months before performance – cancelled a concert with a program possible only for him. I spoke to three or four different people, trying to find someone suitable to take the concert. None of them could undertake it. So I left the problem to our musicians; I'm sure they will have the solution when I go back. It is possible to create a new structure, other models for working together.

ISAAC STERN: There are two points I would like you all to think about. One: what do the orchestral managers think are the possibilities of ameliorating the tyranny of union rules, so often binding in freedom of work preparation and time and cost? I think we have all had the experience, particularly in recording sessions, to hear in the middle of a phrase 'time up, finished,' or 'I'm sorry, but you went three seconds over – we're now in overtime.'

Two, and central to any discussion of the orchestra: how many hours a week for how many weeks can a musician concentrate and work well? This is central to how many weeks a conductor spends with his orchestra, how many programs he has to prepare in the elongated seasons and number of subscription weeks, in addition to the extra concerts that have to be prepared. What is an ideal maximum number of hours per week for the working man in an orchestra, for concentrated work? If we are going to discuss the optimum orchestra, as a working mechanism, these two areas have to be addressed eventually.

HANS ULRICH SCHMID: The education of orchestras, of musicians and conductors and audience and orchestra managers and boards of directors has been talked about. The only profession not touched in terms of education is that of the concert manager. Often we are blamed for the programming failures: the world complains that we always offer the same things. But whenever we've tried to escape the usual way of programming, we've had very bad experiences. Positioned between the orchestra and the local presenter, we have to sell an orchestra and we also have to sell a program. It's always very difficult to get out a program, be it from a conductor or an orchestra manager.

I often ask myself, 'Who is really responsible for programming? Is it the conductor or is it the orchestra manager?' In some cases, it's absolutely the music director who decides: this will be the program, this will not be the program. In other cases, orchestra managers are influential. It's interesting: when an American orchestra comes to Europe the first thing it insists on is that it will not raise such sponsorship in order to perform Penderecki or pieces by Boulez. They want to come and present themselves as an orchestra in the grand tradition, to be heard in the usual Classical and Romantic repertoire.

The BBC Symphony Orchestra, which has to deliver to its audience from a tour every day or every other day, is an exception. As an institution, it is devoted to contemporary music. There you get out very interesting programs. But it's also true that certain contemporary programs can only be sold by certain people. To give two examples: if the BBC Symphony Orchestra presented a contemporary program, it happened partly because Pierre Boulez was the conductor. A few years ago, we played the Schoenberg Piano Concerto on tour, which I would never have dared to do if Alfred Brendel was not prepared to perform the work. No one would have bought that program if not for the attraction of his playing.

PETER PASTREICH: I'm delighted to hear Mr Schmid plead for

interesting new types of programming for an orchestra on tour. My understanding from him, although it's not his view but the presenters', is that we have to be much more conservative on tour than we are at home. When we have, on a number of occasions, put forward ideas for certain contemporary American works on our programs, they have been resolutely refused. In fact, we're about to do a tour under Mr Schmid's able management for which we proposed two fairly major American works, and nobody would buy them.

Ameliorating the tyranny of union rules which are binding us is a new subject and a serious one, but I think the example given is not necessarily a good one. No recording session would end prematurely if we just said beforehand that we're willing to pay overtime. It is a question of money rather than of union rules. The same is true for rehearsals. If we just said to the orchestra 'keep on playing as long as the conductor is conducting, we'll pay,' the rehearsals would simply go into overtime. If I were an orchestra player, I would see that as an issue of money and not union rule.

ISAAC STERN: I wish it were, but it is not. There are orchestras where overtime is available if they want it, but invariably they don't and walk out. That has happened and very recently. The imposition of the rules is a union problem. But I will exempt recordings from this.

May I suggest that problems with programs on the road, while interesting, are not really basic to our discussion of the orchestra as an institution. How does it exist, how it could exist, might it exist better. To that end, one could ask a question: would any of you choose to live where you do if that city did not have an orchestra as part of its central life? That is one of the first questions if one is to discuss whether the orchestra is going to ossify and disappear.

ALEXANDER GOEHR: I am quite prepared to live in a city and see the orchestra die if indeed it is doing nothing of substance and value. I don't support the notion of live music at all costs, preferring to listen to mechanical music or gramophone records if the content of what is offered live is not worth bothering with – as, I'm afraid, is often the case. The problems mentioned by Mr Baechi and supported by Mr Schmid are, of course, quite real, and well known to all of us. But they were presented as statements of defeat, the statements of those who have tried and lost. Success is the ultimate, crucial issue. The problem here is very much a deeper one than is generally assessed. I don't know whether it has anything to do with education; I would say it has more to do with flair. Round the world, the so-called experimental element in a season of conservative and otherwise rather desultory concerts – cooked up by enquiring suggestions of a number of conductors or soloists whom the orchestra wishes to employ – is a gesture of conscience, rightly turned down by the public. The Third Symphony of Lutoslawski seems to have appeared rather frequently and in various places recently. This has nothing to do with anything I have to say about Mr Lutoslawski, but the piece is offered in appeasement.

The basic problem is that the seasons as a whole are not planned organically. My experience comes largely from observing, at a slight distance, the dismal situation in London as it has been for a number of years – with the noble exception of the BBC Orchestra, which works under totally different conditions. One orchestra kills another orchestra; you observe, not that there aren't interesting pieces being performed throughout the year, but that there is a lack of overall thought. If we composers wrote our music the way program builders build their programs, it would be perplexing, even incomprehensible. Priorities are not given serious thought. There are few serious ideas about what one ought to represent in a season: one is despising the audience, and they react accordingly.

Nobody, in the great days of Sir Laurence Olivier, rang up and said, 'Dear Larry, what are you playing this year? ... Okay, so *Hamlet* in the theatre here, *Hamlet* in the theatre there.' Superficially or profoundly, some attempt was made to create a total pattern which represented a point of view, and so had a logic of its own. In orchestra concerts the profession is decayed: it's not centrally concentrated on the repertoire, but built around the artists and their problems. Great as these problems may be, there will be no solution until the planning is based on the work which it is the duty of the orchestra to perform. Then you can go about solving other issues that have been raised. If the music is not first set at the center, you're floundering; no conclusion will make any kind of sense. Nor will the Jeremiah-like pessimism of the managers of orchestras in various towns, who have had bad experiences, ever be changed. They will always get worse and worse. In the end, those orchestras ought to disappear. I shall be quite happy to live without them.

LILIAN HOCHHAUSER: Mr Goehr gives a minimalist's point of view: what does he intend to do with the vast number of audiences who do attend popular concerts? Are they to be denied that, to avoid the orchestras playing the same programs again? The BBC Symphony Orchestra plays what are truly successful programs, but one must face their very low attendances in England, which would be confirmed by anyone connected with the orchestra. One could despise the Sunday evening popular concerts, but there are a lot of people who get pleasure from them, and they should not be denied this pleasure – quite apart from the fact that I like putting them on.

ALEXANDER GOEHR: But in suggesting that programs should be thoughtfully planned, far be it from me to take anything away from the Sunday evening orchestra. I did not mean to propose that the plan should be to play only works by Pierre Boulez or, preferably, myself. By all means, let the Sunday orchestra be. They're not under discussion because they're going on quite happily and successfully. We're discussing the central planning of the season, not what it consists of.

LILIAN HOCHHAUSER: But if you do plan everything, you leave no room for chaos. And if you do eliminate orchestras, you take away possibilities. We don't know the future of our orchestras, but they're all fully engaged. You may not agree with the programs, but nevertheless a great many people want to listen to them – and that's what orchestras exist for.

ALEXANDER GOEHR: I was merely responding to Isaac Stern and I said I didn't care whether they existed or not.

ISAAC STERN: You're perfectly entitled, but I think you're in a minority in this case.

GORDON GETTY: In this company of professionals, there's a natural bias towards modernism rather than the more conservative approach. I would like to speak as devil's advocate for the moment, on behalf of the latter.

I don't agree that today's programming is too conservative; I don't agree that the audience is being despised. We might arguably criticize management for lacking leadership, but it isn't reasonable to criticize them for lacking responsiveness to the audience. The recording industry is one powerful gauge of audience taste; by monitoring what is bought, symphony managers keep up to date on listeners' tastes. Based on what the consumer seems to want, although the future of the symphony orchestra may ultimately depend upon an infusion of new music and a revival of the audience's interest in contemporary music, the symphony orchestra can go on playing Beethoven and Brahms for a long time to come and still have a big crowd in attendance, enjoying it hugely. Audiences purchase records of Beethoven and Brahms in great quantity; someone who has five different versions of Beethoven's Fifth may buy a sixth. We can agree that it would be better if audiences were not apathetic about contemporary music, even if we disagree about the causes, but for the moment our most faithful audience seems to be a conservative one.

I'm not sure that the symphony managers are doing the wrong thing. I suspect that audiences do want new music and we writers of new music could do a better job of running it. Maybe we will come to a grand synthesis through these discussions, but even if all we do is see the other side of the coin, if we hear a surprising view, or an expected view from a surprising quarter, this conference will be a very useful one.

PETER DIAMAND: The speech given by Miss Lindal provoked a great deal of reaction – I would dare to say unanimous approval – and in the very interesting discussions that ensued, provoked passionate outbursts. Is it your wish, Mr Chairman, that we leave it at that? We just take note of it? Or, do you think it could be useful to discuss Miss Lindal's suggestions and proposals in greater detail?

PIERRE BOULEZ: As a realist, I would very much like to concoct a season with you before we leave: an example of a season as you conceive it, with such and such a repertoire, which conductors, the events and flexibility of a real season. Otherwise, it will always be pious wishes, and 'I would like this,' and 'I would like that and, ideally, it should be like this.' We should all sit down together and try to put together a season – even a half-season.

MICHAL SMOIRA-COHN: It is a marvelous idea, if it's possible, to put up a small working party to discuss this. I want to remind you of one point raised in Miss Lindal's paper: that the orchestra be broken up into different groups. This is a very important point at the moment; conductors have many different views on the subject.

PIERRE BOULEZ: That's not a new idea. In the BBC, we divided the orchestra into two and gave parallel concerts for a week. Of course, the unions come into the picture here. In New York, for four or six weeks we divided the orchestra into two parts; I think the musicians were very happy with that. Once we even made three orchestras out of one, and it worked very well. At first, I met with quite a lot of – not anxiety, but resistance to splitting the orchestra. The musicians were very careful, asking 'Where do we go from here? Are we exploited or is this interesting?' Finally, they recognized that it was much more interesting for them to have these split weeks than to have the full orchestra the whole time. In New York, we looked carefully with the personnel manager at the way we divided the orchestra; there were complaints – 'Last year you didn't put me in the chamber orchestra; this year I want to be there.' String players said that they could hear themselves at last. We should try to achieve the flexibility that will allow us to bring to the orchestra both individuality and collective responsibility.

ISAAC STERN: The questions of programming and divisions within the orchestra go together. Even on the same program, they're divided. Why not have a sextet in the same evening a symphony is played and break the routines and break the rhythms? It's something that I find terribly attractive, knowing that no organization has ever dared really try.

NICHOLAS SNOWMAN: Splitting up concerts between orchestras is something we're also exploring – with the London Philharmonic, the Sinfonietta, the Academy of St Martin-in-the-Fields. The different musical forces in that city are all working together now at the South Bank; in the near future, we can abolish the old-fashioned one-off: one concert after another without any rhyme or reason. In fact, the 1988–9 season is broken down into five very separate festival seasons which include the whole of the South Bank, and take in theatre, cinema, music. Our discussions include Peter Hall, the National Film Theatre, the Hayward Gallery and the music world, trying to put some sense into the London anarchy. To help make this work, we're giving orchestras first bite of the dates if they take part in different seasons. We then guarantee them, before all other promoters, use of the Festival Hall for their own events, which, of course, are the one-off concerts which they wish to do and which are often linked to recordings. The orchestras really do feel they have their own home. It's only after thematic concerts and the orchestras' own promotions have been taken care of that everybody else comes in. That produces, more or less, a season that's fifty per cent thematic concert giving.

We hope to raise sufficient sponsorship to be able to encourage orchestras in taking risks they otherwise would be unable to take. Orchestras are often maligned. I was surprised to find, when I was recently back in London, the degree of cooperation they gave to more complicated programs. A sponsorship program helps the orchestras with the difference between what is called an ordinary deficit and a special deficit incurred by putting on a piece by Schoenberg, for example. Fundamentally, the idea is to avoid what Alexander Goehr aptly called the duty piece, the piece you insert for your conscience. Contemporary music, contemporary painting, contemporary everything should be part of a general theme in a natural way, in the way life is lived, and not as a due paid to some moment of conscience.

Regarding orchestral touring, I'm a little disappointed in my friend Hans Ulrich's pessimism. He knows very well, I hope, that there will be changes. Suffice it to say that a number of orchestras in America and in Great Britain wish to take part in these themes, which will incorporate orchestras from all over the world, and not just come in with Mahler's Fifth. They want to take risks, and have asked to do so. Orchestras are meeting together, trying to incorporate themes, as are orchestras internationally. There's a general feeling that we are moving in a sound direction. This is not being done against anyone's will, but in league with the live musical forces of the city.

HENRI DUTILLEUX: It is very difficult to say anything now that so many of you have expressed your ideas. But one thing strikes me: the need to create and defend music written in our own day. Promoting contemporary music is clearly at the center of everyone's thoughts. In the final analysis, could one not paraphrase Schoenberg, that 'music is not modern, it is badly played'? The whole question is contained in this famous remark. A lot of contemporary music, to use this terminology, is very well played. In that case, all is well. At present an audience is being formed. You have spoken a lot about training orchestral artists, and I think it's more or less the same problem for us, the composers. If we don't convince the orchestral musicians of the need to play this new music and the music still to come, which is not yet written, which is created every day, if we don't give them this kind of training, how can we communicate with the audience?

Recordings & Contemporary Music

JOHN RUSHBY-SMITH: Although I do work for the BBC, I also produce gramophone records, and perhaps find my greatest stimulation in that arena. In fact, I've called my paper 'Recording and Contemporary Music.' Mr Fleischmann referred to that industry as a scourge. We must not forget however that, far from keeping audiences away from concerts, the gramophone record has been a major force in educating the public; in certain cases such as France-Musique or BBC Radio 3, network broadcasting is also. Working as a Tonmeister with the BBC Symphony Orchestra, I find many of the problems already touched on familiar. Some of them are raised again in this paper, which also identifies two areas where money is needed and would be extremely well spent. If I speak of London, then it is because it is the musical center of which I have the most direct personal experience.

Because it is a radio orchestra, the BBC Symphony's repertoire is vast. It includes a high proportion of contemporary music, much of which has been specially commissioned by the BBC. The orchestra enjoys a reputation as one of the finest vehicles for contemporary orchestral music – no small thanks to six years working under Pierre Boulez. It is also one of the fastest orchestras, when it comes to learning new works, which makes it very economical in terms of rehearsal time. It is a malleable orchestra, and the quality of its performance reflects accurately the quality of the direction from the podium – something of a mixed blessing, since it works with many conductors, and any shortcomings can be reflected in performance with attendant damage to the orchestra's reputation and morale. This demonstrates, perhaps, why some orchestral members talk about the tyranny of the conductor: there is nothing worse than an inept tyrant. At its best, however, the BBC Symphony Orchestra ranks among the world's great orchestras, especially when performing twentieth-century music.

The orchestra has made several successful gramophone recordings, but unfortunately the commercial market for the repertoire at which it excels is limited. Few of the major record companies are prepared to put their resources into recording obscure works or contemporary music, since it is hard to justify such investment commercially. Often extravagantly scored and demanding more rehearsal time than conventional repertoire, contemporary music is costly to produce, often prohibitively so when viewed against likely market returns. This means that an important slice of orchestral repertoire is less than well represented in the gramophone catalogues. Important because unless orchestras perform modern works, it will be increasingly difficult to justify their continued existence in the modern world. Without a contemporary repertoire, orchestras will eventually be seen as part of a museum culture, and an expensive part, increasingly under threat as less labor-intensive musical media, using electronic synthesizers and the like, take over public taste.

Already, musicians feel the economic pinch as they find their grip on the world of commercial music weakened by the technology of Yamaha or Moog. The reduction in the number of opportunities to pick up lucrative commercial engagements on the side, as it were, means that the musical profession is becoming less attractive to youngsters looking for a career. That's speaking from a financial point of view. Because the chances of having their work issued commercially are slim, so long as they write for conventional forces, more and more composers are turning to electronics as their preferred medium.

Small labels can afford to issue recordings of contemporary works that don't cost much to produce, and composers can even make their own recordings, only needing a marketing organization for distribution and requiring relatively small sales to cover costs. But these small labels can't afford to finance orchestral recordings, whose session and production costs run into several tens of thousands of pounds. It is my contention that gramophone recordings and broadcasts, far from eroding audiences for live concerts, actually stimulate public interest. And a sound base of contemporary repertoire on record can only serve to encourage public attendance at concerts featuring such repertoire.

As I see it then, there is a major opening for some sort of charitable foundation to support the recording of contemporary music – indeed, of twentieth-century music as a whole. Such support could take the form of grants to existing record companies, subject, of course, to stringent supervision. But better still, a new label could be established, complete with its own marketing organization, to issue recordings of twentieth-century music, recorded by performers of the highest international reputation and prestige and engineered to the highest technical standards. Ideally, such an organization should have its own production and technical resources, though initially this wouldn't be necessary since high-quality facilities, certainly in most European cities, are available for hire when required. Subject to negotiating new terms with the unions, especially in England, it ought also to be possible to issue recordings of major public concerts, thus spiking the guns of the pirates who make such a good living from taping and transferring prestigious radio broadcasts without paying a penny to the performers. Whether such recordings are issued would then be decided retrospectively in the light of performance success, and the knowledge that extra revenue might accrue from an engagement could sharpen players' concentration considerably.

From here my paper goes on to discuss the provision of suitable recording venues, something we may get on to later in this discussion.

SEMYON BYCHKOV: We're talking about programming; this is very challenging, perhaps the most crucial responsibility a musical director has. Not only do you program your own concerts, but you oversee a symphony orchestra's entire artistic activity. It's extremely important to perform new music – and all the composers I've spoken to have agreed that they wish their music to be performed with the same commitment, integrity, preparation and effort which goes into performing, say, a Beethoven symphony. It would be productive if we considered the conditions under which symphony orchestras operate, the particular rehearsal conditions and all the regulations that often prevent the musicians achieving their desired artistic results.

For that matter, as much as I appreciate the importance of bringing popular classical music to the audiences, we have to be careful of instant music making. No less time should be invested in the performance of a Beethoven symphony than in one of a piece of unfamiliar music. That's where the danger lies. We're so quick to capitalize on the fact that the audience will attend and the box office will be happy that we forget that this doesn't mean we're developing an audience: we bring their expectations to the level of the performance. It doesn't do the music any good, it doesn't benefit the audiences and it corrupts the performers who have to play the work every day, day in, day out.

ISAAC STERN: Many people – conductors, administrators, even

audiences – are suffering from ennui: here we go again, the same thing over and over. To be perfectly blunt, the ability to get an idea across from performer to audience, to give life, to give creation to the composer, is a special talent, and not as general as one would like to see. There's not one of you, as conductor or composer, performer or music administrator, who has not been galvanized by the force of intellect, personality and personal belief of this conductor, that pianist, this violinist, that singer or that composer. It's the talent to dominate, and this is really why the stage exists. You cannot consider the presentation of music simply as a matter of habit or of social acceptance. Music doesn't come to life except when it is needed, and that need is activated by those capable of dominating the listener with what they believe to be true. That's where the final answer lies for me.

How do we free musicians so that they can operate at an optimum, so that music can always be something special in the lives of performer and listener alike? As Rostropovich put it, rather succinctly and accurately, every concert must be an event. Every performance can be, at its best, a premiere. No one country's concerts are ever alike. The air is not the same. The listeners are not quite the same. Those who are performing do not feel the same. They have different attitudes from one performance to another. In a very real sense, every performance is a first. The question then for us is, how do we free the members of the orchestra and those who work with them, so that they can give the conductor the very best possible instrument with which to realize his talents, to give him the kind of strength and color that makes it possible for him to be free?

I've heard, and I have performed with, orchestras with less than first-rate conductors. When the orchestra had pride, when they had a tradition, when the musicians were well trained, no matter who was up there they kept up their standards. When orchestral players are inspired to great performance by the conductor or the soloist, or the circumstances or the music, something electric happens. How can we experience those magic moments more regularly in the concert hall? Rather than spewing out day after day, week after week, month after month, season after season, one concert after another like a row of sausages. This is a problem that we have all come to know and recognize. How do we take the concert out of the realm of an everyday job and into that of unique experience?

Suggestions were made of how to achieve this. One, about programming, was to have different formations playing different kinds of music. I would like to address a question to the composers, the conductors and the orchestral musicians, those who've had direct experience playing music. Do you believe that it is necessary or better to have one group of performers specifically trained in the immediate contemporary music, music written within the last ten years? One forgets how much of what we consider classic is actually twentieth century. Or do you think that a good, well-trained musician should be able to play all forms of music – contemporary, Baroque, Classical?

PIERRE BOULEZ: Certainly a musician should know all the repertoire and be able to perform Baroque music, Romantic music, Classical and contemporary music, but there is a diversity in personalities which does not allow one person to play every kind of music. Specialization is, more or less, a necessity. If musicians are involved in the music of the fifteenth century, that will be studied in depth, in order to perform in accordance with the truth of the text. We live in a period in which authenticity plays a large role. Until now, music was adapted to the present: the performances of Furtwängler were more or less Wagnerized Beethoven. We now have an historical view, with authenticity as the first goal. Beethoven's Third Symphony must be played exactly as it was at its first performance to qualify as an authentic performance – although I think that's going too far, to the point where authenticity becomes its opposite.

A musician who has researched the fifteenth century and that period's style of playing is too involved to develop a very good knowledge of other musics. So much information is available on each subject that a certain amount of specialization is a necessity. The trend is not towards a centralized organism but a pool of organisms; those who are flexible enough can go from one to another. Groups can play together or offer separate events related to each specialty.

The Orchestre de Paris and my own Ensemble Inter-

Contemporain are experimenting together. We shall work on concerts at the same time, but separately. The Orchestre de Paris will prepare some pieces, the Ensemble will prepare others and they will be mixed in various programs. Thus the two facets of twentieth-century music will be explored: the more classical and the more experimental.

The audience can be highly specialized as well; some frequent opera-goers never go to concerts. When I was with the New York Philharmonic, I introduced choral works, which I consider very important in the literature, but we had protests from listeners who wanted to hear the instruments of music and not vocal music. The orchestra could remain the center of everything – but I'm sure it will not. We cannot escape a future era of specialization and diversity.

ISAAC STERN: Thank you, Pierre. Just as a point of order: this does not answer the simple question of the orchestra itself as an organism. Offshoots, whether members of the orchestra or not, will occur wherever there is musical enquiry of informed people. But what do you do with the two hundred years of the central core of music? That period, roughly from 1750 to 1950, by which musicians' qualities as musicians are judged, not only by listeners and critics but by their peers, musicians in the craft. This is the largest body of creativity we have at this moment; it has lived on continuously. Also, do you feel that a truly well-trained musician cannot be well informed by those who have specialized, and who are willing to share their knowledge and experience with a musician who has not been able to delve as deeply into each of these areas but is willing to learn?

PIERRE BOULEZ: Of course, any musician who has goodwill can learn quite a lot; more and more, the nonspecialist will learn from the specialist. But musicians have to choose, more or less, their principal activity in the orchestra's life – where they sometimes go as they would to a factory or an office, where they have security but do not enjoy the employment, going outside to other jobs for pleasure. I find this terribly disappointing.

A first horn must have great pleasure in playing Mahler's

Fifth – he has a big solo in the third movement. But the eighth desk violin does not hear himself at all for an hour and a quarter, and it's not very rewarding. Playing a Haydn symphony, in a very reduced orchestra, he has much more pleasure as well as time to look at the phrasing and so on. If he plays *Pierrot Lunaire* with the orchestra's soloists, or Berg's Chamber Concerto with wind instruments, he finds something more refined. With the orchestra, you have to solve problems quickly, efficiently, but you cannot solve everything. You try to find the best compromise. You may have five or six rehearsals, but you may only have three, and then you have to feed this machine in the short time allowed. That is frustrating. It's not satisfying for the conductor, who knows he cannot really achieve perfection, nor is it satisfying for the musicians. In chamber music, you have fewer of these problems, because each individual is more concerned, more responsible; it goes quicker and into more depth.

The orchestra's geography is another problem, which I touched on yesterday. Mr X plays near Mr Y for months, even years; as in an old marriage, people understand each other very well, but the relationship may be daily on the verge of collapse. If configurations are changed, the individual relationships, created progressively over time, are changed. But if the entire organization were more flexible, so would be the musician's mentality. This evolution from different historical periods, from chamber groups to bigger groups, will bring vitality to the life of an orchestra. It's a practical problem which managers can solve much better than I. The question is: do we have to have various groups which mix from time to time for special events, or can we have one central group from which different responsibilities are distributed according to that year's program?

ISAAC STERN: Thank you, Pierre. I know there are some who want to comment right away, but before they do I am exercising the privilege of the chair. You still have not answered the central question which I asked before: the orchestra itself. Does it remain a viable organism that should be somehow remolded? Not split off but remolded and in the best possible way we can conceive. Not to get caught in the day-to-day pits, whether this one enjoys being next to that one or not – there are always going to be human problems.

I'm aiming at a definition of the symphony orchestra as we know it. Implicit in what you had to say is something which has to do with the funding of orchestras in general: there are too many concerts and too few rehearsals. The priorities are completely wrong. All the effort goes into trying to produce a product in the shortest possible time which leads to the compromises Mr Bychkov spoke of. There are ways, but we're not sure we can realize them. We may not reach the ideal necessary direction, but I'm talking about the orchestra ... Let the performers speak first.

SEMYON BYCHKOV: Flexibility is the critical key. It does exist, more in some orchestras and less in others, depending on the union regulations and the size of the orchestra. Having ensembles within the orchestra is not something new. The Grand Rapids Symphony, which I conducted for five years, has exactly this set-up. It's an original orchestra, and therefore plays ten pairs of subscription concerts. It also plays a number of concerts outside the subscription system, but maybe fifty per cent of the time spent working goes into chamber music. There is a core orchestra, the permanent, fixed ensemble, about forty-five strong, and an augmented orchestra for the subscription concerts. You can have a couple of string quartets, a woodwind quintet, a brass quartet, you can have a piano trio and ensembles that are not fixed but created for a particular repertoire or purpose. It benefitted the orchestra's development particularly. People had not only the opportunity but the challenge to practice, to work, to deal with repertoire otherwise inaccessible to them.

That is relatively easy to do in an orchestra of that size. It would be a logistical nightmare to work out with a major orchestra of one hundred players – but some way has to be found if the musicians are to reacquire some raison d'être. The assembly line, a way of life and a practical necessity for producing concerts, contradicts the special events we are all looking for. Not only the critics, but every performer, every one of us hopes that each performance we give is an event, at least in our own lives, and when it stops being an event, we are in the wrong business. We should quit it altogether. Some way – affordable, logistically possible, defying union-imposed limitations – must be found, to allow flexibility for a different kind of music making in a different environment.

As to whether this should be a permanent group split into units, or whether different, specializing groups should be brought together to perform symphonic music: I believe that a permanent symphony orchestra is necessary to provide the continuity of people playing together all the time. In great orchestras, you have it; in chamber music, you have it. People feed each other; they need to feel completely at ease, knowing what everybody else is doing – it doesn't matter whether it's forty musicians or one hundred, playing a Brahms or a Mahler symphony, the idea is still the same. That only comes from working consistently with one another. Whether this is done with fifty per cent chamber-music playing and fifty per cent symphonic literature or with very different percentages, is open to discussion.

GARY BERTINI: The orchestra as an instrument, as a form of expression of music, is viable and will be so in the future. Our discussion should not question its existence but try to discover, out of our own experiences, the points that could be improved. Small improvements can always be made, but these are things of major importance. Changes occur in the orchestra's life simply through the reality of musical life, the life of society and the composers who in their works express a need for the orchestra to stretch itself and change. The structure of what we today call the symphony orchestra could be used for many other imaginative things; it depends on the leadership and the attitude of the musicians – which has to start being developed during their preparation and education.

I find contradictions in some of the remarks made. One I would like to point out is that between musicians' necessary specialization and the public. We complain that the public wants to listen to a symphonic work; they don't want to hear a choral work; they want to hear a contemporary piece; they don't want to hear a Classical piece; they want to hear a Baroque piece, played authentically; they don't want to hear Romantic pieces or contemporary pieces anymore. We have to find a way to retain specialization without separation into more and more small groups playing for ever-smaller groups of people.

Chamber music is, and must remain, a privilege and function of musicians' free interplay. Pierre made a valid point, citing the string player who says, 'When I'm playing Haydn, I can hear myself, I can regulate, I can develop more, and I enjoy it.' But the field of chamber music as such, the orchestra's most flexible structure, will and must remain the free choice of the musician. By nature, an orchestral group, of 20 musicians or 120, will always be led in this or that form. The musician will look for a way to express himself. It may be possible to link the orchestral structure with the benefits of flexibility, while keeping the continuity of tradition of composition from the Classical and Romantic periods into the new music.

ANNA LINDAL: I agree very much with Mr Boulez, especially as he relates his artistic experience in splitting the orchestra. As an orchestral musician, it is something I long for: to bring into the orchestra the special interests, that real joy of music making which usually takes place outside it.

One always says the orchestra is an unwieldy institution, and it is, it's difficult to change, but I do think that by going ahead and doing something like this, different answers and different reactions to these proposals would soon appear. Most musicians would not be against changing to more creative procedures. Chamber music will always be done outside the orchestra too, but within the orchestra, the Schoenberg Concerto and other twentieth-century pieces which are not often performed could be given. But the change will not be initiated by the musicians themselves.

When one speaks of specialization, the specialist in Romantic music is never mentioned. It isn't necessary; everyone's a specialist in Romantic music. For contemporary music and Baroque playing, it's clear more time is needed.

PIERRE BOULEZ: By using the word specialization, I don't mean to imply that music is literally like the medical profession, where there is a kidney specialist and a knee specialist and so on. But if you are playing music of the fifteenth century, you

have to spend time and find ways to perform this music again.
You cannot say, 'Oh! I'm a genius. I can always play it the
same way.' In the nineteenth century, that may have been
possible. It isn't any longer. For the most part musicians have
not received the proper education for authentic performance,
so far as the word authentic has any meaning, satisfying
performances of music from between the fifteenth and eighteenth centuries. The necessary knowledge is deeper than that
generally acquired.

In contemporary music, especially when the composers are
developing new ways to approach performance, you have to
learn a great deal: it's living material, and progresses each time
a composer writes a new composition. You have to know more
or less what the composer wants. In my old days at Darmstadt,
every composer thought that he had found the best method of
notation; for each ten pages of score, you had to read through
perhaps fifteen pages of notes about notation. You can imagine
the amount of work implied, before even beginning to read
some scores. Some forms of music demand more time; for
the bulk of music we generally speak about, when you have
received your education, you're supposed to know how Schumann is performed, how Brahms is performed.

GARY BERTINI: All this is absolutely correct, but I think we
know of many performers and orchestras who play Brahms
marvelously but don't play Haydn so well.

FREDERICK ZENONE: As an orchestral player, and as someone
very happy and very proud to be one, I think our workplace
can be changed for the better of the player, the public and the
audience. In my ideal orchestral world, one comes in as a
generalist and spends one's life in the orchestra as a generalist.
What is wrong is to expect to take in 'educated musicians,'
and then each week and each month for forty years break a
piece of that education off and use it up. The institution itself
doesn't take responsibility for the performer's education over
time.

We should look carefully at revising some historical models –
for instance the Leipzig Gewandhaus, where any number of
discrete ensembles come together to make a very respectable

orchestra. Maybe there is a model we can learn from, whereby one can become, so to speak, a specialist in areas of interest, depending on one's career stage, development, education or need. It's not to say that someone who is interested for the moment in Baroque music will remain in that niche for the rest of his time in an orchestra, or one who chooses to play new music will become so specialized as to do that for an entire life. One's education continues and it can embrace many things.

In the player's free prerogative with regard to chamber music may lie answers to our problem of flexibility. Experience leads me to believe that the musician in the orchestra perceives that when the organization asks for flexibility, it asks for flexibility for itself, not for the player. The player must remain free to make some of those choices – with whom does one play chamber music and how does one play it – which can't be dictated under the general umbrella of the institution's flexibility. It's this kind of thing that gets us into polar positions, from which our problems seem insoluble.

One final observation. For the past two days, I've heard a lot about orchestras; in between, I get the uncomfortable feeling that when we talk about orchestras generally, we mean the New York or London experience. The experience of the orchestra is much, much broader. Many orchestras in the Western world would not accept either of those experiences as representative; I would only caution us all not to accept them as models.

ERNEST FLEISCHMANN: I would like to answer Isaac Stern's original questions with the words 'yes, but.' Yes, the orchestra is able to be the central musical organization of a community, but it has to do a great deal to justify that position. Yes indeed, every musician belonging to an orchestra should be able to play music of different periods with a great deal of competence and quality, but we have to recognize that within any large number of musicians are many individuals.

I hope you'll forgive me if I quote from my own experience. We asked those members of our orchestra who are particularly keen to play contemporary music, to join a pool known as the Los Angeles Philharmonic New Music Group. We've asked those who are excited by chamber music to join the Los Angeles Philharmonic Chamber Music Society. Some of those overlap. Obviously, we expect that everyone, by virtue of having auditioned for and been accepted into a major symphony orchestra, is capable of playing the total repertoire. In response to Mr Bychkov's statement that a major orchestra will have more difficulties than a regional one in creating that fragmentation and total service: that may be, but it's up to management to provide for its musicians. It's up to management to provide for its audience as well, and offer to each of them the widest possible musical experience, so they can derive the greatest benefits from each other.

For a program which included a Mozart and a Haydn symphony, as well as the fragments from *Wozzeck* and the closing scene of *Capriccio*, not only did splitting the Haydn and Mozart orchestra halfway down the middle with strings and winds enable us to have twice the number of rehearsals, it gave every musician – and a lot of them commented on this, every string player certainly – an opportunity to play Haydn and Mozart, and rehearse them extremely well. We have to give a great deal of consideration to how we do this, to work a little harder at it if we hope to become, as we should and could, a total musical resource for the community and for our musicians. It is not an impossibility. It makes for a more complete orchestra. It makes, in the end, for a better orchestra.

Incidentally, in answer to Fred Zenone, we do not dictate to our musicians that they belong to any of the groups. It is entirely on a voluntary basis. Their work, as part of the new music group or the chamber music society, is on days when they are not working with the Philharmonic and they do it happily. Of course, they are paid extra for it, too, and that's only as it should be.

It is true we should not only deal with New York and London. Is it possible, as a result of this conference, to form a study group to look into the various types of structures that exist and perhaps come up with a proposal for an ideal structure from which we might all benefit?

PIERRE VOZLINSKY: I have, of course, been listening with a good deal of attention to everything said; it appears that, for certain historical reasons, I must be the only person here who has created an orchestra the principal aim of which was precisely to be able to produce an infinite number of groups. I may say, in passing, that I'm sorry that Gilbert Am, whose idea it was to create the orchestra, is not here; he was unable to make it, but I'll speak for both of us.

When we first had the idea of setting up an orchestra that would be infinitely divisible, there was, of course, a good deal of opposition from the unions. This opposition has now been overcome. Perhaps because of this example, I know of no symphony orchestra in France where, for reasons of structure or of union intervention, it is impossible to remove a particular group of players to perform a particular work. Having said that, I would point out that certain things have become merged which, for me, are quite separate: groups and chamber music. The dividing line is drawn by the work that the orchestra does: a group, however small, needs a conductor to perform a work; groups without a conductor are part of chamber music, which is a totally different issue. The former automatically comes within the scope of orchestral services. It also creates problems of organization which can be extremely complex, and even prevent the orchestra from operating smoothly. In return, some fundamental questions must be asked concerning chamber music. Should musicians who play chamber music be paid for that by the orchestra? Or to the contrary, should that preparation time be deducted from their salaries? Or should they be sent off on leave, for others to emulate? These things may seem down-to-earth, but there's no point in philosophizing: it's this that we, as the people responsible, have to sort out.

I'll give you an example. A string trio, the Trio de France, who were in the Orchestre National, specialized for the most part in contemporary music. A lot of works were written for them in France. Over the years, these young people showed a great deal of courage: in addition to their regular work, at some personal cost, they built up a reputation and a repertoire as a trio. Well, at a certain moment, they managed to obtain their release from the orchestra, while continuing to be paid by Radio France. Thanks to the Ministry of Foreign Affairs, they were able to go and play all over the world, while remain-

ing bound to the orchestra which could integrate them more
or less whenever they wanted. This shift, which can't be
ignored, deserves to be studied. It's true, if rather sad to admit,
that if a group of chamber musicians is too successful, there's
bound to be a problem within the orchestra. For my own part,
I sincerely hope they make the most of it, but I know it will be
a problem, and that they may end up leaving the orchestra.
Hypothetically, that would be a solution – but at a cost of three
good players. The transition period in such a case would be
extremely difficult to handle, because the continual absences
will be an obstacle to the smooth running of the orchestra. At
the same time, our code of ethics as musicians persuades us to
help them.

To come back to what I was saying at the beginning. On the
problem of flexibility and size: with a normal-sized orchestra
this flexibility cannot be taken too far. We made extremely
precise calculations *before* creating the orchestra; it continued
to run perfectly smoothly. I might even say it made considerable progress, in being allowed to perform the Classical
and Romantic repertoire. We came up with 136 musicians
which, of course, is not commonly found, but with that number
you can play virtually everything all the time.

ALEXANDER GOEHR: I'm going to be guilty of Mr Zenone's
correct observation that a lot of the discussion is based roughly
on a London-New York model; this may not apply to a city
with limited resources. I also intend, if possible, to address
directly the chairman's initial question: whether or not the
orchestra, as it exists now, really cannot in our opinion
continue. But I want to do so in a slightly polemical and
dissident manner.

It's an historical commonplace that movements of opinion
or policies often achieve the exact contrary of their settled
goals. There's no policy pleading for greater rigidity in the
orchestra; everyone agrees that there should be flexibility,
educational possibility and variety. We are practical people;
we don't spend much time considering the theoretical impli-
cations of the things we discuss. However, an element of that
plan, which has found widespread echo, takes underlying
theories for granted.

We talk about fifteenth-century music, Baroque music, contemporary music – but Pierre Boulez is actually talking about the repertoire of the Ensemble InterContemporain as if it were the repertoire of the whole world. If tomorrow a composer appears who needs a different kind of ensemble, which doesn't have the particular experience of the Ensemble Inter-Contemporain, presumably one either decides the music is no good, and not to have it, or creates yet another ensemble to specialize in that?

What lurks behind a lot of this discussion is a plea for the increase of the orchestra's power and influence. There is a confusion here. On the one hand, we have the notion of a city-state: many people of different views create different kinds of organizations and limit each organizational structure to what they can usefully do and no more – a traditional model of city existence. On the other hand, we have very real dissatisfactions among orchestral musicians. So those reorganizers of the orchestra should take over, it is said. The Ensemble Inter-Contemporain, the London Sinfonietta, all those ensembles which are independently financed and independently managed, should be run by the board of management in the interest of the orchestral musicians. Though the intentions are noble, is this not possibly the wrong way to set about it? Is one not trying to make an empire of the orchestra? The orchestra should be limited to what orchestras are paid to do, and there should be money available for other organizations to exist, with their own disciplines and their own structures. It is not implicit that the orchestras should solve the problems which have been pointed out, because it could only result in an extension of the power of the manager. And managerial virtuosity, while a wonderful thing, might also be subject to limitation.

KARSTEN WITT: The question was whether in an ideal world the orchestra should be split up. If we are discussing the question this way, we have dissent; otherwise, we would probably have a consensus. Let us look at various situations. The audience wants a broad repertoire regularly performed and they want to be able to learn, which means it has to be possible to go deeper into a special area: a special composer, time, theme. The composer wants original interpretations, the possibility of new forms of interpretation, new works, interesting programs.

The ideal world which Isaac Stern was probably speaking about was the world of the interpreter, no matter what repertoire, no matter which audience and no matter what his own capability; the ideal interpreter wants to do everything which normally is not possible. How to behave in this situation will change with different groups of musicians. For example, Steve Reich's ensemble, as far as I know, does not consist of broadly talented musicians who can do anything. They have specialized, they have worked a lot in this area and now that's their means of existing in the world.

In London there are all sorts of groups of musicians; the individual musicians may change in these different groups, each one of which has to work very efficiently. With the minimum of rehearsals you want the best results, so you have specialized musicians who do the same again and again; they almost only need to sit together to play what they always have. In Regensburg the orchestra has to provide the entire musical services for the region, which means that the musicians have to teach at the children's music school, go to the schools and speak, perform chamber music and play in the orchestra. And everything is organized by the orchestra itself because there is no other organization; there is no manager other than the one employed for this job by the city.

I don't think we should wait until the end of this conference to have a study group look more closely at the different situations. As far as the theoretical problems are concerned, we have probably touched most of them, and there appears to be a consensus about our goals.

BASIL TSCHAIKOV: I'd like to start by saying that, for a lifetime, I have been happy as an orchestral musician. I have been happy as a general practitioner, and during that time have had the joy of working in innumerable specializations. I have worked on Beethoven where people have brought a Wagnerian approach and with those who brought a twentieth-century approach, with people like Bruno Walter and with Mr Boulez. I've had the joy of playing a Strauss polka, which I found as rewarding musically as working with specialists on the Schoenberg Chamber Symphony. I've worked in every sort of music. I've played light music. I've enjoyed playing with Mr Mantovani and standing in front of a little microphone and playing 'Charmaine' backed by forty string players. There's a joy in playing that music if you play the clarinet. I have played all the music for the clarinet written from 1700 to 1979, when I stopped playing professionally. During that time, I found it a totally rewarding experience.

May I say, and I hope this doesn't sound pretentious, I found it a wholly rewarding experience because I like music and I like people and the way in which I reveal my liking for people is by playing music to them. If they want to hear me play a Strauss waltz or a Strauss polka, I hope that I can do it and I hope that all of us would want to do it with the same degree of integrity as we would a piece by Mr Boulez or Mr Beethoven or Mr Schumann. I have done work on Schumann and Brahms, having played their symphonies for thirty years, and have found it as rewarding as playing a piece I have never played before. This is part of being a human being. You make life interesting by your contact with it. I find it interesting being here with you, gentlemen, although a number of you hold views which I think I am very much in disagreement with. There is no one who has spoken so far, since I've been here, that I've thought boring or I haven't thought worthwhile. One makes one's life.

I agree completely with Mr Goehr. The orchestra is not the only place. The sort of instruments played in an orchestra, however they are played, whether in a fifteenth- or twentieth-century manner, are not the only sort of musical instruments. There exists immensely rich music played on instruments whose names we don't even know. There are so many African musics, Indian, Chinese, Japanese, American; there's a whole wealth of experience that if one could have three times as long as one is allowed by nature, one would still only be scratching the surface. So, to be unhappy and bored as an orchestral musician seems to me not to be a problem of society but to be a problem of the individual.

The individual is the product of his time, his age, his culture. We bring young musicians up to have expectations which cannot be fulfilled. Most of us are brought up to think that we are going to be another Heifetz – in my case, another Reginald Kell. Most of us will be good workmanlike musicians, whether conductors or instrumentalists.

Let us recognize other needs, other groups of musicians, other ways of making music. Recognizing that, does the orchestra in the latter part of the twentieth century enable those people who want to play in it to do so with dignity, in a life-enhancing way? I would say no. Not unless they are troublesome people, rebellious, able to make decisions, unwilling to do what they're told – in short, bloody nuisances. An orchestra made up entirely of that sort of person would be chaos. But if you are not that sort of person, the right circumstances do not exist. We do not give people in the orchestra a sufficient sense of dignity, allow them to make decisions, or choices, or see themselves as responsible for the way the orchestra functions. And I speak, if I may say so, as someone who has worked in every sort of orchestra and been the chairman of the Philharmonic Orchestra, the equivalent of being a company's chairman of the board: I made decisions about who conducted, what was played, who played ... So I have tasted power. I know what it is like to enjoy those possibilities. I also know what it's like to play with people no one should play with. And what I would suggest is this: we need to enable the orchestral musician to realize an ongoing education, responding to the same needs as all other members of society do. We ought not to think about that person as a mere commodity.

Orchestral musicians care, as much as any critic, any conductor, any manager. As Charles Munch said, if you want to find someone who loves music, look for the guy who's sat at the back of a symphony orchestra for thirty years among the violins. If he didn't like music, he wouldn't be able to tolerate it. Very easy up at the front: everyone's clapping, saying how good you are. Bloody difficult to go out there day after day and give of your all with the same degree of integrity as if you're playing a concerto. Gentlemen, I beseech you. Don't let's just talk about The Orchestra: think about the people in an orchestra, who play because there are people who want to be excited and have their lives enriched. That's what we're here for.

Otherwise, it seems to me that we're doing nothing except inflating our own egos.

ISAAC STERN: Thank you, Mr Tschaikov. Very well said. One hundred twenty-six Tschaikovs in our orchestras and our problems would be over.

GARY BERTINI: Different sorts of orchestras are playing now. When we discuss the theoretical subdivision of an orchestra doing a Haydn symphony with half of the orchestra, and on the same program, a Mozart with the other half, we should realize that there are many such orchestras. I have been the musical director of two such orchestras, where by union rules, by the contract and regulations, you cannot split the orchestra. If you want, you can do a Haydn symphony with a quarter of the orchestra – but it is considered that every rehearsal uses the services of the entire orchestra. Which means you pay everybody, and you can't do it. This exists in many countries and in many cities. This is one aspect to consider, if we all decide that flexibility in terms of division is necessary. We have to speak of the imposed realities.

ISAAC STERN: Those are some of the problems which will have to be answered once we strike some accord about the correct approach as regards rehearsing and paying the musicians. If they're rehearsing different things at the same time, they are providing their services – which amounts to the same thing.

GARY BERTINI: No, it does not. I'm sorry, but that was my point. You pay it twice ...

PIERRE VOZLINSKY: We've touched on a basic problem. It shows that there are attitudes, or rather customs, in the world which set unions and professionals in opposition. I'm a bit disappointed and surprised to hear that there still exist systems that force people to pay for a service which isn't in fact performed.

In France there was a similar system: the conductor could very well be working with only a small number of players, but it was counted as a full call. Since 1975, since the disappearance of the ORTF and the creation of Radio France, this system has been completely swept away. It was that which allowed us to create the new Orchestre Philharmonique where there is an individual breakdown of the musicians. But at the Orchestre de Paris, where they haven't had these changes, there's also an individual breakdown. In spite of the fact that the unions in France are not exactly inactive, this basis for payment is clearly admitted.

ERNEST FLEISCHMANN: May I just make one suggestion? That Mr Boulez join the union Mr Bertini speaks of. Most times when he comes to conduct our orchestras, he has four rehearsals in one day with four different groups; but if his fee therefore needs to be quadrupled, that union is something we should all join.

HANS LANDESMANN: I unfortunately have to agree with Mr Bertini. In Vienna, particularly with the Vienna Symphony Orchestra, the situation is exactly the same. We have to pay the entire orchestra even if they work in small sections; if they do two sectionals at the same time, we have to pay the entire orchestra two times over. As far as I know, this is also valid for the Chicago Symphony. It was rehearsing *Wozzeck*, the guitarist was just doing the piece with the singer – a little scene – and they had to pay the entire orchestra for that one scene with the guitar player. It's a famous example.

But, I really wanted to make a different point. Again coming back to the Vienna situation. The Vienna Symphony Orchestra has eleven different music groups working within the orchestra. The Concentus Musicus is probably the best known with Harnoncourt. There are four or five chamber music groups and there is one modern group. Unfortunately, what it now amounts to is a constant fight between management and these groups, because they take away so much time. At present they can't work as much as they want to, because the management won't let them, needing their services for the entire symphonic repertoire. It's a double-edged sword: we encourage the musicians to do extra work, but we don't give them the time to do it.

PIERRE VOZLINSKY: Where this is concerned – and it's a basic problem for the orchestra's survival – we are in general much too discreet and too modest when we speak to our paymasters. Who pays for the orchestras? The local or national party in office, or private consortia? If we have the courage to explain to them that their money is being badly used, since we cannot obtain normal working conditions – by 'normal' I mean not paying someone who doesn't work – the person providing the fees may well say 'If things don't change, I'll stop the money.' There will be a lively little crisis, but a relatively short one, and the situation will be resolved.

CHRISTOPHER BISHOP: Anybody looking in here from outside would find this very odd. Here we are talking about a symphony orchestra, which in a way takes a long time to build up, like a great cathedral – and we're trying to divide it into apartments. It would seem peculiar, but of course the reason is the players themselves do need to feel that they are other than just symphonic players. It's extremely tedious to sit playing symphonic music all the time. The difference between Regensburg and London – forgive me, but one can only talk from one's experience – couldn't be more extreme. In London, you have every possible contemporary group and you have groups playing old music and chaps who can play crumhorns, sackbuts and nakers. In Regensburg everything has to come out of the orchestra, as it must have been in Bach or Haydn's time. In the middle we have a place like Los Angeles, where Mr Fleischmann has obviously managed to get an admirable degree of separation, allowing some of his players to go and do separate things.

Of course, there is the danger that these separate organizations take on lives of their own. If that starts to happen, it can be very dangerous indeed for the orchestra. The best players might all disappear. It would be lovely to have this world where everybody knows different things about music. I would very much like to form madrigal groups out of the Philharmonia; the more madrigals they sang, the better in tune they'd play. One day, when we have enough money, we shall do this, but it's rather like angels dancing on the head of a pin. We must be very careful to look at practicalities. The best possible solution is to give your players as much performing of small works within the concert program as possible. It's also much nicer to start with a work rather than the overture, to start with a Haydn symphony – than which there is nothing more disciplinary. And if you are going to play Mahler or something overblown in the second half, it does at least mean that the audience's appetite has been whetted. All orchestras should play at least ten Haydn symphonies every single season.

PETER HEYWORTH: The simile of trying to divide a cathedral into an apartment block is not quite what was suggested. To me it seems to be more like a cathedral with chapels. People are not trying to break up the orchestra entirely. Mr Bishop also mentioned bringing a too successful group to a sharp end; the Berlin Octet were, I think, all members of the Berlin Philharmonic, which was able to wear their success perfectly well.

CHRISTOPHER BISHOP: That's a different kettle of fish. The Berlin Philharmonic has twice the number of players the Philharmonia has. If you have a very large orchestra, in which some members play some of the time, it can be done. But if the whole orchestra has to play all the time, and you only have one principal oboe and one lead violin, a chamber orchestra will destroy the actual orchestra. In the comfortable world of Berlin, things are very different from Regensburg and London.

ISAAC STERN: If we are here to discuss a possible future, it is obvious that no artistic entity can exist as a business. It has to be funded. The extent to which it is funded is the extent to which society recognizes, and is willing to undertake, its responsibilities. If we could find a way to instill excitement into that body of artistic endeavor, there might be more willingness on the part of private societies, in some countries, and public groups in others.

The search for money is a partial cause of many problems we've been talking about. It has (a) created a much larger budget because of the extended season length in many areas; (b) created a terrifying ogre of producing for the funder, producing therefore more and more at less and less of a standard; and (c) it changes the character of the organism to what pleases the greatest number of people in the shortest possible space in time – the antithesis of any artistic progress. Artistic progress is not made through general acceptance, but by the leadership of the farsighted ones who will insist under difficult circumstances to go ahead and bring up the level, generation by generation.

NICHOLAS SNOWMAN: Having lived in France and now returning to London, it is interesting to witness the debate over dividing up this ridiculously small cake, which I think is 0.5 per cent of the national budget. In France, it was 0.48 per cent and was then doubled to 0.96 per cent, I think, under the last government. In Great Britain, I talked to a lot of people about this, including MPs. The argument there is that the country must be made aware of the political value of cultural activity, if I can put it that way. The idea has not yet caught on in Britain. There are votes in concerts; there are votes in cultural investment. That point has been made in France.

Without talking too long about Jack Lang, at one point that political history is interesting: when it became clear that the last government was going to lose the legislative election, Lang's popularity was fifty-one per cent. The country wanted him to remain minister whatever government came in, which of course is nonsense. But that kind of official government commitment to giving over a reasonable part of the national budget to cultural projects, plus taking legal action to make it easier for the private sector to donate, which has just happened in Great Britain, have to be brought together in order to make things work. In Britain, a new law has just come in which ought to be helpful, but when there's a political realization of culture's political power, there will be less talk about who's going to get which bit. Is it ENO or Covent Garden? Who'll get the 0.94% increase, though inflation's at 4.8%? The discussion should be on doubling the budget. Only political action can make that clear, a major, all-party campaign. There's a long way to go. In France, that work has been done; there, however, the Conseil d'État won't allow the tax law which would make other things possible. Each has something to offer the other.

ISAAC STERN: It might be worthwhile later on for those

involved to look at some joint action in the European community, not only nationally. I can only report in terms of the USA, where we've had secondary governmental support through tax deductibility for artistic enterprises for a long time – some thirty years or so. And the curious thing is, the government – we call it the National Endowment for the Arts, which I had a hand in helping to create during the Johnson administration – has raised the level from a paltry $9 million to about $156 million. Because of that stamp of approval, a recognition of the national need for arts funding, the private sector has increased their contributions over the past ten years from approximately $250 million to something over $600 or $700 million a year. Between the two, there's $900 million year in one form or another going into the arts – and this at a time when a fiercely anti-intellectual and anti-supportive administration has tried very hard to cut back on all support for the arts. Despite that, a small group in Congress has staunchly maintained the level at least. This doesn't keep up with the inflation spiral and constant rise in cost of operating, but at least funds have not been cut. The value is recognized.

Parenthetically, if I may tell you a story which exemplifies the idea of art as useful, of a community growing around an orchestra: in a defunct area in a city called Rolling, North Carolina, they rebuilt an old theatre. Within two years, knowing there would be concerts, orchestra, ballet, more than $400 million of new construction went in; a downtown area was revived simply because an arts facility became available. The tie between a performing group and the city around it is evident. How we use it is up to our talent and intelligence, but that an art center does make a whole community prosper is something you cannot question anymore. It is visible and provable.

KARSTEN WITT: In Germany, the whole world of music is so institutionalized that it's not possible to debate an ideal situation. The money we have is money from the government; the government will only give the money to institutions which already exist. We have to talk instead about how to change these institutions. Twelve years ago, we started to build up a new organization in Germany, the Philharmonic; now we have two professional orchestras in that organization. Although we are extremely successful both within and outside Germany, even today we don't have any money from the government. Nothing. The situation for our people is clear: almost everybody goes into one of the existing professional orchestras. The only way to change this is to offer a concrete challenge to the practice. Although we are trying to do something new, ours is a unique situation which won't really apply to other orchestras.

ISAAC STERN: This touches one of the subjects we've mentioned before, the preparation of musicians. There are so many differences – different countries, different orchestras, different views as to how these ideas and values can be applied, that we should frame an ideal artistic approach, realizing the practical necessities of local application. You speak of the problems in Germany, but that country is also held up as an example, given the number of opera houses, the quality of playing in the Berlin Philharmonic, etc. The same thing in Vienna is different. The Vienna Philharmonic is almost entirely self-governing, self-operating, with an old tradition which it maintains, over and over, at a very high standard. There are many ways to apply a basic ideal; it may be considered that we can devise nothing, certainly in this short time, to fit all circumstances. The surrounding structure will vary, but we can devise an approach and the basic, necessary elements within the organism, elements that will tend, within any framework, to develop a living, exciting structure. That in turn might induce others, whether from private, government or business sectors of society, to come and help. We can outline ideas that might be offered others to think about while they support their own institutions in their own way.

Every organization that has an interest in continuing its future or being part of a continuing future is going to have to learn its way around the political world; that's part of the responsibility of being in a public society and part of something we all have to learn.

HANS LANDESMANN: I've realized during this discussion that in each country the individual needs – whether of the orchestral musician, the composer or the public – are amazingly similar. What we heard from Sweden could apply to all Europe and America; the behavior of the public seems to be, with certain small differences, very much the same. We should work together towards an ideal which each individual country or organization can then try to approximate, by its own means, implementing the governmental, union or sponsoring changes its situation demands.

PIERRE BOULEZ: I come back to what I originally said: it depends essentially upon the dimensions of the city. I'm sure the solutions for New York are not at all the same as the solutions for Regensburg. I've come to this extreme: either you have a central organization, which can split and go in various directions according to what you want to program, or you have immense forces scattered throughout a city which are not joined in a single organization. The more forces there are, the more specialized groups exist, which can merge from time to time for special operations but which have independent lives. I'm sure that the size of the population is a capital factor in the organization of a city's musical life.

GARY BERTINI: Numbers or statistics are not always the rule. If I may speak about my own country, with about 3.5 million inhabitants, we have at least one major international orchestra, another symphony orchestra, any number of activities, concerts, a public of thirty-seven thousand subscribers to the Philharmonic in Tel Aviv and eight thousand subscribers in Jerusalem, in addition to the Philharmonic subscribers there. The quality of ideals, the ability to deliver something exciting, depends on leadership, and on education in the wide sense of the word, and the response that we musicians can give to those needs.

ERNEST FLEISCHMANN: There are fundamental differences according to the size of area in which we operate, but we could learn a lot from each other if we took some time to examine what we really expect from our peers and colleagues. What does a conductor expect from a composer, what does a composer expect from a musical organization, from musicians, from soloists, what do you all expect from the orchestra's management? We often seem unclear about our respective functions and interrelationships. Might an examination of this help us to find some way towards, if not an ideal solution, the structure in which the future of the orchestra can flourish?

BASIL TSCHAIKOV: If in any country we want society to support the orchestra, would any of you find the suggestion acceptable that we conceive of the orchestra as a resource center? This is an extension of the idea that we break the orchestra up, which immediately and emotionally we are unhappy about. Rather, we could think of this group of players as serving the community in a variety of ways.

Let us think of a group of something like 120 to 130 people, general practitioners but some will like playing contemporary music more than they like playing Schumann and Brahms. There are several orchestras in the world where musicians who usually play their violins and cellos pick up Baroque instruments for several weeks each year. In some cases, they've proved themselves to be of exceptional quality; the group in Cologne has made records considered comparable to those by any other specialist group. This is not the only thing musicians want to do: they want to teach, to write, to be involved in the community, perhaps as *animateurs*, stimulating other sorts of music, where they interact with children, with those who have played in youth orchestras and have learned instruments while they were still at school.

Something like this could be tried, for example, in the southern part of England, where the Bournemouth orchestras have had great problems. They already have two orchestras, a symphony orchestra and the Sinfonietta. They have the right number of players. That group of players could be put together as a total group and used in a rich variety of ways, allowing people to be general musicians – I think that is our normal condition – and also to do other things. It's a starting point.

To take up what Peter Heyworth said, if we think of the orchestra as a large, beautiful building broken into a lot of flatlets, we would be making a big mistake. But if we do think of the orchestra as a cathedral in which there is room for many chapels, there is room within this large organization – which has proved itself now for two hundred years – to stimulate composers and produce a sort of music that tens of millions of people have never heard before. We should be thinking about this in an absolutely positive way.

Somebody said we're complaining that there isn't enough money, that musicians don't enjoy themselves. One thing has sustained me throughout forty-odd years: I wear my badge of service in the orchestra as a badge of honor; it is something of which I am immensely proud. I am unhappy to see so many people associated with the orchestra who aren't proud. This may be a way forward.

KARSTEN WITT: The wishes we have for the orchestra have been articulated; now it is a matter of sitting down and putting them together. I would warn however against taking the suggestions made as something to be immediately put into practice, relying on technocratic expedience. I was horrified to hear about a computer being used to organize the different musicians into groups by interest. This is a technocrat's vision, someone who must think a pool of musicians can somehow be split into ensembles on paper and something relevant will follow of itself. Musicians themselves have to choose with whom they play, and they have to choose the program, at least when they play without a conductor. This idea of putting orchestras together is also very dangerous, because every ensemble has to have its own identity. Identity, of the small group and the large, is the real problem in splitting up the orchestra. I have hundreds of questions for people who have experienced this.

If you invest much money and time in one group, you want to work for the identity of your own group, not only for that of the whole ensemble. If smaller ensembles are given the larger group's name, one must be sure they can sustain the quality which the whole group has. The Berlin Philharmonic Orchestra has a rule: groups of more than thirteen players may not use the name Berlin Philharmonic as it might then be supposed that this is a part of the orchestra itself.

CATHERINE FRENCH: In the USA, we probably have two or three hundred part-time professional orchestras; in some cities, they may be only ten or fifteen miles apart. And despite current difficulties, of funding and everything else, efforts to combine those orchestras have, by and large, not been successful. There's only been one merger in the past twenty years. In many cases, the same musicians play in these different orchestras. I don't know the reasons. Some of it has to do with boards, with city pride and with community pride. Some of it has to do with resistance from the musicians. We have maybe forty or fifty orchestras of the size Mr Bychkov was discussing, like the Grand Rapids Symphony. He described the good conditions, the possible ensemble work. In some communities however, the other side of that is apparent: playing at every shopping mall, supermarket opening and hotel opening to provide enough work and bring enough income to the orchestra. Let's talk to those players about artistic experiences. I hear an awful lot about what we are going to do *to* the musicians. We're going to change the orchestras, cut them up into various sizes, but I don't think we know enough yet about what's important to the musicians, how they feel about this.

PIERRE BOULEZ: What is destructive is to play fifty-two weeks, concert after concert, in exactly the same way, the kind of routine where one week cannot be distinguished from another, or one day from the next. The musicians at the New York Philharmonic were happier when for some weeks they split, when they found themselves in a smaller group, when they found something different, when there was a different atmosphere. Simply that. I can assure you the results were positive; this is not just wishful thinking. The routine must be broken from time to time, with events of some kind, even just a change in programming, or the grouping, using a different setting or different activities. From time to time I would explain the works with examples given; the orchestra was very interested in this kind of thing because it broke with the repetition they had in their normal life.

PETER PASTREICH: I have difficulty with the concept that 'routine' means playing the same kind of things and 'interesting' means playing different kinds of things in different groups. Everyone knows that routine means playing with boring conductors and playing in a boring way. With the right musical direction, it doesn't have to be routine, even if one's playing twenty weeks of subscription concerts in a row. The wrong person would make playing all kinds of different things every week boring. Of course, some variation is useful, but it won't solve the basic problem.

FREDERICK ZENONE: When I referred to my orchestra and the way the ensembles work, I suppose it was understood that those ensembles were created by the management and music director, who assigned people to play with each other. But none of that was the case. The musicians themselves decided who they would like to play with; they each chose a name for their quintet or quartet. The role I played as musical director was simply advisory; as far as the repertoire was concerned, it was done in their own concerts, for their own series. They would say, We want to play these pieces, this is what we want to play for different ensembles, and would you give your opinion as to how they would fit into a particular program? It was very beneficial for me – I was involved in programming areas I wouldn't usually deal with. That was the extent of my involvement as musical director; the rest was done by the musicians. Of course, chamber music is still a privilege for musicians to do on their own, but it can be done under the umbrella of a symphony orchestra.

ANNA LINDAL: I would like to repeat what we have heard before: Mr Boulez will soon be invited to join another union. He speaks very well for the musicians. I have a specific wish; I should imagine Mr Boulez did as well, when he worked with the BBC or in New York. He wanted to do more contemporary music, and this may be the only way to have the musicians specialize in this kind of music. You just have to decide whether or not you are interested in developing this, and whether the artistic directors of the orchestra are interested.

FREDERICK ZENONE: We've been drawn a bit off center, the discussion fragmented as a result of some quantitive mis-understanding about what is being said. None of us wishes to pull down the symphony orchestra. Certainly Mr Boulez's experience in New York concerned the symphony orchestra, and this, I hope, is what we are all talking about. We are not presenting the orchestra as some kind of employment agency to satisfy the whims of its employees, but trying to engender a situation that will broaden the orchestra's experience and speak directly to a city's performance needs – the city where the orchestra lives, after all. This cannot be done in a vacuum.

PIERRE VOZLINSKY: I'll be even briefer. I'd like this meeting to adopt a resolution which commits each of its participants – assuming this is not already the case – to mount a campaign in his or her own country to the end that an individual breakdown of musicians be adopted there. Without this, none of the ideas put forward here can ever be properly implemented.

CHRISTOPHER BISHOP: We've found a very satisfactory way, as I'm sure, have others, to give the musicians – the string quartets, the brass groups and so on, which form themselves out of the orchestra – an outlet. The Friends of the Philharmonia host concerts as fundraising or social evenings, and engage these players, who often play for nothing – which shows what kind of musical, rather than financial, incentives motivate them. We do about four of these a year, and they are immensely successful, attended by all the people who support the orchestra.

PETER HEYWORTH: We may be reaching a central point, coming to it from two directions. We've talked today a great deal about fulfilling the lives of orchestral players; that, in a sense, is the internal working of an orchestra. But we talked about another point yesterday: enabling the orchestra to react to the demands of the moment, particularly in the field of contemporary music. An orchestra is an economic entity. Too many industries in Britain have in the past existed purely for the contentment of the people engaged. An orchestra must respond to the challenges of its time. Fortunately, this central point we're reaching is that, in the process of making life more varied for orchestral players, the orchestra will actually be making itself better prepared to meet the new and differing challenges that face it.

ISAAC STERN: Thank you, Mr Heyworth. We've only touched peripherally on two other aspects of this: the relationship of the orchestra to the city in which it exists, or how to make a bond between music-makers and the people who live around them; and the training of young musicians.

ERNEST FLEISCHMANN: Peter Heyworth has well presented the point that by helping to make the musicians' lives more interesting, we improve that of the musical community. In order to develop this larger repertoire, this larger service both to our institutions and the communities they serve, I really do think we should pay some attention to enabling that community to change from passive into active participants – to become perceptive audiences.

ISAAC STERN: Alfred Brendel, as a performer, you haven't said anything about your sometime colleagues. Would you like to have a word about them?

ALFRED BRENDEL: What I have to say is completely unconnected with anything that has been said here so far. As you know, I have played with orchestras but not in an orchestra. I realize that in this company I am marginal, apart from sometimes being able to fill a hole. I usually try to be my own orchestra; even without the orchestra's existence, I could lead a rather heavy, self-contained life, thanks to the incomparable literature for piano alone. Yet, I would sorely miss orchestras and I have learned more from them and from conductors than from pianos and pianists. As a soloist, I have found most conductors very helpful – at least, those under seventy – and orchestral musicians much more interested in music than in their reputations. I think I know my obligations toward an orchestra. What I want to talk about is the obligation of the orchestra towards the soloist. I hasten to say that not always are all of them met, particularly if the pianist is young and does not draw the crowds.

First, there should be enough time to talk to the conductor and to rehearse with the orchestra. The conductor should not be treated as an improvization. There are few soloists and few conductors who do not enjoy rehearsals – one can see them as exceptions. Rehearsal time depends on the piece. Mozart needs more time than is often granted; for this reason in the fifties and sixties, when I lived in Vienna, orchestras rarely performed his concertos. In the case of Mozart, no union regulations or public demands should prevent the orchestra being scaled down in size for the occasion.

Second, the pianist should be offered the time and proper facilities to select a piano, get acquainted with it and work with the tuner if he and the condition of the instrument require it. He should be able to rely on very good instruments from which to choose, and he should choose on stage: to try out instruments in the basement or storage room is usually quite misleading. He should have some time to himself with the instrument and the tuner. It should be the orchestra's responsibility to provide this, yet in very busy halls the soloist finds himself fighting, not always successfully, for a chance to go through his cadenzas and do the necessary voicing with the tuner. Again, there may be a few colleagues who do not care how well a piano is tuned or voiced. They are eccentrics, fired by the sentence, 'There are no bad pianos, only bad pianists' – which remains wishful thinking.

This brings me to the maintenance of pianos. It is not enough to select an excellent Steinway these days and put it up in the hall. To keep it in excellent shape, a great deal depends on the quality of the tuner. Unfortunately, the piano technicians employed by the orchestra are not always of the standard a good pianist should take for granted. In my experience, collaboration with a first-class technician is always easy; it's just that there are so few of them. I could name some important cities where not even the tuning is up to standard, not to mention the fine art of voicing and regulating. A lot of damage can be done by crude voicing, which takes the substance of the sound instead of improving its quality. There is a much greater shortage of truly professional tuners than of pianists. The profession of the concert tuner has to be encouraged, I would almost say at all costs. A few music schools, like the Vienna Academy, run classes for piano mechanics. There should be a much wider pool of young aspiring specialists, from which, one hopes, a larger number of excellent concert tuners would emerge. I'm delighted that recently some ladies have taken up the profession.

In a time when the price of pianos is constantly rising, while the quality of material and craftsmanship, compared with fifty years ago, is in decline, the care instruments get is more crucial than ever. I'm not sure that all orchestras in concert halls realize this or act accordingly. The profession of a tuner and a piano mechanic needs to be sponsored: master-classes should be held; young men and women who have shown some musically mechanical qualification should be helped financially. With the exception of a few top specialists, the profession is underpaid. Piano literature is not for nothing the most wonderful literature for any instrument. A decline in the standard of instruments may well result in a decline of musical artists.

ISAAC STERN: Thank you. Very well said, Alfred. I've been well trained in that subject by my colleagues, the pianists I've played with; they say, You carry that piece of wood and can take it with you everywhere; look what we have to work with! I suppose it's only in Japan that they take ten hours to do a tuning, and sometimes two days, and the technicians are trained for ten years before being allowed to touch a piano on the outside, and only one out of a hundred who apply for the job is chosen. They do pay them well, and you can really go anywhere in Japan and get a very fine piano, very well balanced to this day. I wish I could say the same in New York.

Before I ask the gentlemen to read the three papers still left on our schedule, Mr Goehr has asked permission to speak for four minutes. He wishes to make some observations on the events that have taken place up till now.

ALEXANDER GOEHR: Thank you, Mr Chairman. I have to admit to a slight despair at what's been said here. I've heard a great deal about flexibility, organizational innovation and virtuosity and almost nothing about music. Only you, Mr Chairman, referred once to the different ways of getting from one note to another, and Mr Witt has referred to the musically significant notion of a community among orchestral musicians. The problems of orchestral musicians, their alleged weariness with their dull task, have been frequently repeated. We could equally well meet and discuss the frustrations and disappointments of the Chinese peasantry or Detroit car workers. In every place where fiscal reality prevails, routine, mediocrity and boredom are norms of human activity.

So it is in musical institutions. Only a child believes you can institutionalize excellence. The belief is only possible if one thinks that excellence is the result of purely material conditions: spend more money, buy better players, build better facilities and 'Hey, presto, we're in heaven!' But the greatest musical experiences of my life have almost invariably been in lesser circumstances. All this is really about the humble love of music, and its complexity, and the occasional ability of a group of people to overcome these complexities and make a statement about an individual piece.

If musicians find that uninteresting, if the public doesn't want it, then let them go discover something they do find interesting. We can only talk about orchestral practice and innovation if we recognize that our purpose here is to achieve an excellence, which by its nature must be unique. It is the classical literature's complexity that makes it relevant to us and to our publics. It is the canon, the temple of which we are the acolytes. The young composer must struggle to be admitted even once to this temple. For my own part, the highest artistic moments are to see the perplexity on the faces of the audience in, let's say, Leningrad, at a performance of one of my pieces and then their release from that perplexity when, afterwards, a piece by Mozart is played, because I seek a platform to measure myself against the great masters, to confront the lovers of this great classical music with my own pitiful efforts. This demands not flexibility but a temple dedicated to excellence – and that's what's exciting about our art.

The eighth-desk violinist, much discussed here, is not a lout who makes noise, but a sensitive and educated person. He or she can recognize when the true aspiration, which recognizes the right to fail, is replaced by the jet-setting personality cult. He or she knows when an artist is serving music and when using it for his own, often shady, purposes. You have talked about this eighth-desk person as if he had no other function than to make a noise, but he too is an acolyte at the ceremony of music. Mr Boulez talks about events as if they were not a ceremony. What is music when it is an event? If this acolyte recognizes that a worm has crawled over his altar, that the ceremony that he is participating in is a simulacrum, a fake event, then he and I with him would prefer to lie down with the swine – by which I mean a quiet bar with some whiskey. I do beseech you to keep before you the realities of the world we live in.

Peter Heyworth said at the very beginning that concerts in London were often regrettably very dull. I don't go to many concerts, nor do I listen to synthetic records because I can't keep my mind on the frequently dull events taking place. Let's realize our first duty: to see that our generation can do justice to the great classics, which form the raison d'être of all orchestras. As a composer, I should be forced to go through fire and water to be allowed into their company.

In these statements lie my beliefs about the problems of orchestral management: the primary need to strive for a spiritual excellence in human terms, not measured in purely materialist categories; the unimportance of the trappings, which we in England call 'big time'; and the relevance of new music and its relation to the classical canon. Proposals for practical innovations must be founded on beliefs. The proposals we make here should be founded on a belief in the ideal of service to a great art.

ISAAC STERN: Thank you, Mr Goehr. Very well said. You've anticipated some remarks, albeit somewhat colorfully, in a personal way. But in general, I think you will not find much basic disagreement with what we all think is the reason for which we're here. We all think that music is the main reason. What we're trying to do is make it come back to life.

Ladies and gentlemen, we have three papers that have not yet been presented. I would like to ask the gentlemen to read their papers now and I would ask you to hold any discussion, unless you are so immeasurably moved that you can't contain your enthusiasm, or the other way round, until after the papers are read.

The Youth Orchestra

HANS LANDESMANN: The great surge in the creation of youth orchestras all over the world seems, at first sight, a very positive development. Hardly a week goes by in the important music centers of the world without the announcement of a concert given by a visiting youth orchestra. Local, national and international youth orchestras vie with one another in booking conductors, soloists and concert halls to enlarge their activities.

As the artistic director of two such international organizations, I would like to give a short summary of their structures, activities and goals. The European Community Youth Orchestra was established just about ten years ago, in 1977. Joy and Lionel Bryer had the visionary idea and the necessary ambition and vitality to persuade the EEC that beyond political and economic activities a joint effort should be made to bring talented musicians from the member countries together to create an orchestra of special excellence. They were able to interest Claudio Abbado in their project, together with James Judd as associate musical director, who has been enthusiastically working with the orchestra ever since. About 140 musicians are chosen from auditions of about 1,000 candidates held in the member countries.

To help countries with a less established orchestral tradition, master classes are offered through the year. Tutors for every orchestral instrument are chosen from among the best educators and musicians to work with each section, and twice a year extensive rehearsal periods are planned with subsequent concert tours. Besides Claudio and Judd, conductors of the stature of Bernstein, Barenboim, Karajan, to mention only a few, and soloists such as Pollini, Norman and Ludwig have worked with the orchestra. Projects with Ashkenazy, Leinsdorf and Mehta are now being discussed for the future. Besides the artistic input of Claudio Abbado, the other all-important factor for the success of the EECYO is Joy Bryer's tireless effort to establish the foundation's financial base. A yearly budget of roughly five hundred thousand English pounds is balanced by contributions from the EEC and its member countries. However, private sponsors such as IBM, ITT, Hewlett Packard and others have contributed generously to concert tours.

The second orchestra, just now being established, is the Gustav Mahler Youth Orchestra, based in Vienna. They hope to join forces with youths from countries with similar musical traditions, embodied by Mahler's legacy, whose genius inspired music lovers not only in Vienna, but in Budapest, Ljubljana and in today's Czechoslovakia and Yugoslavia. It is hoped that governments of the countries, at least at the start, will lend financial support; we did succeed in persuading them of the importance of such a joint effort. The first working phase should begin in April of 1987. Claudio Abbado has taken up the position of music director for 1988, and joint concert tours with the ECYO are being negotiated.

The aims of these two international youth orchestras go far beyond endeavoring to offer concerts to audiences already saturated with excellent professional orchestras. Of the great number of youth orchestras, not all, in my opinion, achieve the primary aims they should. It is necessary to define those primary aims, which I would outline as follows:

1 Young musicians of diverse backgrounds should form a community establishing musical as well as human contacts.
2 Under the guidance of excellent musicians, special education in orchestral playing should be offered, including sectional rehearsals.
3 The musicians should know a wide chamber music litera-ture.
4 The orchestra should prepare young musicians for a career in a professional orchestra and increase the orchestral musician's standing and prestige.
5 A number of concert programs, prepared during the rehearsal period, should be offered.

If we accept these aims and this order of importance, we come to the conclusion that some, for reasons that I shall discuss in a minute, reverse the emphasis. The concerts become the starting point, to the neglect of educational and social aspects. In far too many orchestras young musicians are used to fill gaps left by professional groups; they become the tools of managers or even of artists who create the false impression of an idyllic enterprise while embarking on a commercial venture. In some countries, youth orchestras compete to obtain the best musicians, not seldom offering them financial rewards, thus destroying the foundation of the youth orchestra: its idealism.

The crucial work comes in the rehearsal period. During this time the youth receive important incentives and instruction. Before every concert tour, at least two to three weeks' preparation should be allowed. Of course, this involves a great financial burden which many organizations are unwilling to underwrite. Often, facilities are not readily available; the cost of supporting an orchestra of three hundred members, plus staff and artists, is indeed horrendous, particularly as during this time there can be no income from concerts. Many governments and private sponsors have given a helping hand, but still, for many orchestras funds are lacking. This induces managers to curtail rehearsals and accept as many profitable concert engagements as possible – which destroys those ideas which should be in the foreground. The acceptance of two proposals would help youth orchestras improve their work.

One is the establishment of an international organization of youth orchestras, to meet at regular intervals. Some principles then laid down could greatly facilitate the work of each member group, avoiding possible clashes and interferences. A diary of rehearsal periods and tours could be established, and an effective lobby for all common concerns created.

The other is to create a youth music center. This could be a permanent site, including living quarters, recreational facilities, concert hall and rehearsal rooms. The center should be established in a peaceful environment, without the diversions of a big city. Different youth orchestras could take turns working in the center, which should be under professional management. During times such as May and June, when most schools have exam periods, other groups could use the facilities for postgraduate music sessions, sessions for young composers or for young professional orchestras. Ideally it would be in the vicinity of a city with great cultural traditions and an active musical life. In view of the costs entailed, this proposition may sound too idealistic, even unreal. However, is there a more viable investment than working towards a healthier and better-prepared young musical population?

ISAAC STERN: Thank you, Mr Landesmann. As I said before,

when all three papers have been presented, we'll have time for proper discussion and perhaps some direction. I would like to withhold comment until then. Mr Witt, do you have something in preparation which you'd like to say?

KARSTEN WITT: A paper I submitted to you the first day, which summarizes some of the things we have been talking about during the last few days. There are three sections, all of them very short.

Firstly, a preliminary consideration of the present profound structural crisis in the European orchestra as an institution. A product of the nineteenth century, its social structure was demanded by Classical and Romantic scores and has always been characterized by rigid hierarchies. That structure survives to this day, restricting the orchestra to the cultivation of a fossilized repertory and reducing its members, except the conductor and a handful of soloists, to a purely technical role. Various signs of crisis are the consequence. Although orchestras continue to consume the greater part of public funds set aside for musicians, increasingly large parts of the promotional market of classical music, most especially in the areas of early and modern music, are being handed over to smaller and more flexible ensembles. Because of the lack of flexibility – there is that word again! – in working conditions, large parts of the repertoire, involving important compositions, especially twentieth-century works, are excluded by virtue of their unusual forces or playing requirements. Innovative demands on the part of composers, new ways of playing, new forms of notation, together with fundamental changes in ways we interpret music, are rejected by musicians who continue to see themselves as highly specialized technicians.

Faced with instrumentalists' relatively high level of education and expectation, conductors as a rule are overtaxed by their role. Conductorships change hands with increasing frequency. Instead of working out original interpretations, rehearsals are given over simply to playing through works. Established orchestras play very little part these days in the rapid development of forms of communication and presentation characteristic of the contemporary arts. As a result, these orchestras rarely perform outside prestigious concert settings – in regional art centers, for example, or in other alternative venues. Finally, and not only since the triumphal march of the mass media, classical musical life with its ossified rituals has lost a large part of the cultural and intellectual elite, and above all young people, as its audience.

Secondly: objectives. 'An autonomous ensemble' is the subtitle of this section. If the orchestra is to develop as a group of interpreters of classical music and become a creative, versatile institution in terms of media communication, then a new understanding of this institution is necessary. Members of the orchestra must be able to take part in all planning and decision making, if they are to see their work as a contribution to some cultural process. This involves not only having a say·in questions of programming and casting, but also deciding which conductors and soloists are engaged. Only in this way can their place within the group and their subordination to the conductor be functionally understood as an acknowledgement of a rational working principle.

The hierarchical relation of conductor, orchestra and organization must develop into a cooperative one, so that everyone involved has exactly the same opportunity to demonstrate commitment to the institution.

Thirdly, in order to work together responsibly, the musicians must assume not only organizational but artistic coresponsibility. This presupposes a balanced inclusion of works for smaller formations. If the orchestra is repeatedly restructured in various ensembles, specializations must be possible, to enable the evolution of individual learning processes. The orchestra must be large enough to allow variability in casting, repertoire and ways of playing, but small enough to permit an overview of its activities and to prevent the anonymity of the individual member. If the orchestra is seen in this way, as a forum for varied initiatives on the part of its members in every aspect of ensemble playing, its management will no longer be involved in merely ensuring continuous employment, but will encourage projects organized by individual ensembles working towards specific objectives, for which specific forms of rehearsal and performance will have to be developed.

Self-management of internal affairs seems to be a precondition if the orchestra's ensembles are to engage, on one hand, with the composer, and on the other with the audience, in a creative and communicative process. Instead of a constant repertoire and standardized forms of mediation, we shall find a quest for relevant subjects and appropriate means of representation. Only if the musicians themselves are convinced by what they are doing will their work carry conviction. If the art of ensemble playing is to evolve, then a dramaturgy of programming and promotion must be developed, just as cooperation with other artistic forms and media will lead to the acquisition of new means of expression and fields of influence, and the exploitation of novel venues will allow us to experiment with novel ways of perceiving art.

We have discussed all these things over the last few days. What I've said here is very abstract; it will mean something different in each situation. Nevertheless, points in common are shared by all the institutions represented here.

On the practical consequences: if these considerations are correct, the orchestra as an institution is not helped by setting up orchestral schools in which young musicians are merely prepared for the traditional role of the orchestral musician. Nor can there be any question of orchestra academies in which a new generation of instrumentalists is trained from an early age in the ways of playing and the manners that obtain in an orchestra. Rather it is a question of encouraging new initiatives which the musicians themselves must take, and of encouraging institutions to make the necessary space for such initiatives available. The material support for ensembles will then serve first and foremost to strengthen their autonomy, an autonomy which must exist before new forms of work, new methods of interpretation and new kinds of presentation can be developed.

So far there have been far too few international centers, especially in the sense that Herr Landesmann has defined them, where musicians are prepared for orchestral and ensemble playing, and where experiences are exchanged. Such a center, or such centers, should at least fulfill the following: first, collect information on interesting initiatives, projects and programs, and ensure that this information is passed on to those institutions that run orchestras. I am convinced that many initiatives have been taken, even within institutions represented here, about which we know far too little. They would enable us, in our individual situations, to develop new ideas.

Second, organize courses and projects in areas where there are glaring shortcomings – such as orchestral management, something which cannot at present be learned anywhere. Certainly a great deal can be done to ensure that orchestra managers work more effectively and more sensibly.

Third, courses for conductors. We discussed this problem on the first day, and haven't come back to it since then. There are far too few contexts in which conductors make themselves available to pass on their abilities to younger colleagues. Vocational training courses could also be implemented, especially chamber music courses for orchestral musicians, both young and old; and finally vocational training courses in the field of education, an increasing preoccupation with orchestral musicians, for which their conservatory training leaves them far too little prepared.

ISAAC STERN: I'm sorry. We'd be delighted to have it eventually. Do you mind if we just get to Mr Burton's paper and then Mr Fleischmann and then yours? Thank you very much.

Music, Politics & Technology

HUMPHREY BURTON: I'm slightly embarrassed, Mr Chairman; I said that I would write a paper, but instead I have a lot of notes and some rambles, and shall do my best to edit them as I go along.

I react violently to the suggestion that we should spend hours discussing whether the back desk of the third and second fiddle should join forces to play string trios of Mozart: I ask myself, is this really what we should be here for? Aren't we confusing recreation with vocation? Don't we all recognize that most orchestral players are happy if they have good conductors to work with, good salary of course, plenty of time off to do teaching and other things, a foreign tour once or twice a year, some television and recordings to change the rhythm of things? There are more important things which we should be discussing than how to keep an orchestra happy.

If all the concert halls in the world were to be burned down,

probably not more than five per cent of the community would
notice the difference in their daily lives. In many parts of the
Western world, the world which still cares about orchestras,
where orchestral playing still matters, most people don't care
one way or the other about culture. In France, in Britain, in
the United States, we hear only of support being withdrawn.
On Friday, the Arts Council declared that it was not going
forward any more but would be pulling back. Exxon in America
has already pulled back its support for cultural television and
in some places for cultural activities in the orchestral field.
Shopkeeping principles are being applied to art: everything is
expected to pay its way.

Art institutions, opera and ballet companies as well as symphony orchestras, are struggling for funds and suffering
because of it. The Royal Opera House in London offers the sad
spectacle of a beleaguered institution, so busy fighting for
survival that it's neglecting matters of long-term policy.
Support for the arts isn't what one might call a party matter.
Despite Nicholas Snowman's assertions, I don't believe it is a
vote-winning or vote-losing issue. Not even in French politics.
Jack Lang was a popular arts minister, as Jenny Lee was in
England, but both were profoundly uninfluential at election
time.

None of the British parties are committed to raising the level
of public arts subsidy. The Tories want private sponsorship to
replace it, refusing to recognize that private sponsorship after
ten years of Tory government has never come to more than
ten per cent of the total sponsorship in the United Kingdom.
The Labour Party wants more cash for democratic arts, which
one takes to mean street theatre and ethnic pantomime. The
message from the politicians is clear: if you want to find ways
of preserving these marvelous labor-intensive institutions of
yours, like opera and ballet and symphony orchestras, then
you've got to go out and fight for yourselves.

But those who do care, the happy breed, the precious few,
care with boundless passion, as we've heard in the last few
days. I thought that Basil Tschaikov's defense of the status quo
and the kind of orchestras he teaches his youngsters to look
forward to working in, is absolutely remarkable. We're lucky
that we have such people to help our students as they prepare

for the orchestra life. Then we hear from some countries that things are fine. 'Crisis? What crisis?' the Viennese might say. They point to their Philharmonic, where in the golden hall of music, the Musikverein, you can spend half an hour simply applauding Bernstein or Herbert von Karajan. The Viennese may have a more comfortable life than their counterparts in London and Paris, but they are living in a place where music is taken absolutely as part of the central meaning of life, as it is not in the more western outposts of Europe and America.

Passion is also evident, thank goodness, in the Promenades that the BBC organizes over eight weeks in the summer. It seems some mystique is enshrined in a thousand young people listening to the music standing up, promenading as they call it. This boxing arena, this tennis court, the Royal Albert Hall, is turned for eight weeks into a great symphonic center such as Alexander Goehr would like us to have, a temple for high culture. Twelve orchestras, a dozen more conductors take part every year in this fantastic festival. Why is it that the passion can be lit, the flame made to flourish there and not in other parts of the concert-giving world? Ask Ernest to tell us about the Hollywood Bowl Season. Ten weeks, sometimes twelve weeks, seventeen thousand people in a kind of communion with music. The sound is assisted, they say, with stereophonic help from loudspeakers, but it's still, although not a concert-hall experience, a very satisfying experience. There seems to be some intelligent force abroad in a packed musical audience. They are intrigued, bewitched, using it as some sort of religious or mystic experience.

Finally, ask the audiences in the City of Birmingham, a hundred miles from London, why they have got it right; why they have somebody who can create a great sense of occasion? Simon Rattle has created there an orchestra of international force, which has given the city and the whole society there a sense that they have something really worth having. Mainly, the success has to do with his own personality. He has a serious personality, a certain determination to be unglamorous which in a way is itself glamorous. He has taken an example from his neighboring city, Stratford, and refuses to be browbeaten into the belief .that London is the center of everything. The musical director is the key to the problem we've been discussing, the interface between community and orchestra.

One aspect of my work in television has brought me into contact, year by year, with young students, the ones not yet at college. We run a competition with BBC Television called Young Musician of the Year. The top age is eighteen – there's no limit in the other direction, some are as young as ten or twelve. Every year we have at least five hundred youngsters: string players, woodwind players, brass players. An interview is part of the competition; many of them come forward and tell me they want to play in a great orchestra. They have this idealism. They know that it's a worthwhile career.

Music remains an important and valuable career. The wealth of talent we see is more than enough to support symphony orchestras and small ensembles right across the world. We've heard that in America, sixteen thousand youngsters come on to the music market every year. I'd like to ask Isaiah Berlin whether he can give us a philosophical response, given this enormous volume of intake into the musical world, to the paradox that we still have only half a dozen violinists who will sell out a house, why it is that my colleague from Germany told me that he can no longer afford to program a conductor and a soloist in the same concert very often, because they cost too much money? Isn't it strange that we don't have a distribution of talent permitting a wider market in this field of soloists, indeed of conductors? Not only old established orchestras, but new ones like the European Chamber Orchestra and the Junge Philharmonie, can survive if they're well led. Standards are rising, and yet we have discontent. We need an historical perspective to understand this.

When the big orchestras came into existence, we had an industrial society based on the revolution in public transport; later, trains and buses were cheap, which meant that audiences and performers could come together regularly, in large pur-pose-built halls – and there was very little else to do with one's free time. But nowadays, society has dozens of choices for leisure activity. We are having to fight as never before for art to be given its true, as we would say, attention. The spirit of the age is dominated not by industry but by technology. We're being pressured by advertising, which stresses individual aspirations. Even orchestral players are uneasily aware that they are sacrificing their individuality, which makes them uncomfortable since they're told so often by so many media that it's important to go your own way. This society is no longer one based on culture.

I thought I'd bring with me what I take to be musical, the center of my life. It isn't the Royal Festival Hall, it's just this little black box. It isn't the Albert Hall, it's this transistor. Not the acoustics of a great concert hall arena, but these headphones. And my experience is, I believe, the musical experience for ninety per cent of the musical world, to whom advertisements for gramophones and videocassettes and televisions and so on are addressed: these are the things that preoccupy their lives. And if we are going to attract the attention of the younger world, we've got to go the way the world is moving, a technological way. We've got to provide new publics with ways of convincing them that music, performed in public, has something which cannot be achieved in any other way. When I've finished work, I'm urged to go swimming, play squash, to go to the movies, to rent a video, to go and play snooker, and I've got to know if I'm going to a concert that it's something outstandingly special. It's this that orchestral managers have got to face, and there are different ways of handling it. They can reflect this technological spirit as museums are doing: we can turn our concert halls into active places. It's been one of the great revolutions of the eighties that museums are no longer places that have to be laughed at or sneered at; there could be a quite different approach to the way we go to concerts. To take one simple example: wide screens could be placed, as you saw at the Olympics in Los Angeles in 1984, so that you could see – you may be shocked by the horror of it – the hands of the solo violinist, the face of the conductor and his gestures.

Alternatively, or in addition, in front of each audience member's seat the score could be provided, the pages being electronically turned. This is about to be installed in new aeroplane seating; in ten to fifteen years it will be installed in public concert halls. Now, if you find that idea too distasteful, you must go down Boulez's path of creating an event as unlike as possible to listening to music at home. You have to create a total experience, apply theatricality to concerts. It seems so obvious that I can't see why it hasn't been done before. Set the hall in total darkness before the music begins; in that darkness, to hear great actors speaking lines which create a mood before the work begins. The conductor to come on stage ready to start, as he will sometimes in a contemporary opera production. You have to vary the way concerts are presented, in other words.

Recently, at a concert given by the Philharmonic Orchestra at Westminster Abbey, the hall was used in a way of utmost poetic value to the music being played. One should recall Benjamin Britten's memorable speech, delivered twenty years ago: going to a concert should be something very special, something worth saving up for, worth making a special journey for. Concert managements at the moment don't have the slightest notion of how to create a sense of theatre which will make people want to go to a concert. Managements and players have really got to come out to meet the public. The Sinfonietta at the Festival Hall has done something marvelous in that respect, putting on free concerts, open days, free rehearsals, free children's days, anything to get young people into the place.

I don't want to exaggerate the part that television plays in this field, knowing that it's not a particularly important part, but it's been useful. The transistor has been replaced by the microchip; the Walkman has been the most significant development since the long-playing record; television has made enormous technological advances in the last few years. Instead of the enormous 35mm camera that we all worked with five years ago, we have things the size of a small cassette. You can record an hour of high-quality pictures and digital sound. That little box of mine is the realistic music center, and the concert hall is no longer the place where we get all our music making from.

Television has modified the way people experience music, just as radio has. Technically, the television world is getting better. Compact disc recordings, on the whole an improvement on the old style of analogue recording systems, will provide the most wonderful music for audiences of the nineties. But there are more revolutions on the way in the video field. The video disc has the quality of sound associated with the compact disc, and has a superior television-quality picture. You can already buy these in Japan and America, though mass production of this new technology hasn't been perfected. Another development is stereo television. Two loudspeakers will be built into your television set – this is already prevalent in Japan, West Germany and America. It means buying a new television set, but sets are getting cheaper, the screens are getting larger and by the year 2000, stereo television will be something you have as a matter of course.

The third development is that of satellite television. Within a few years, you'll be able to receive pictures and hi-fi sound from all over the world. The pace at which we've changed our method of transmission over the last few years is certainly not going to lessen. A small dish on the top of your apartment or house will be turned up to the sky; fitted with remote control, it will tune into the varying paths of dozens of communication satellites thronging the airlines.

Finally, cable already applies to many countries. Cable, which usually involves packages, played over and over again for weeks on end, encourages the dip-and-mix attitude to culture. You get Verdi's Requiem at two o'clock on Thursdays, eight o'clock on Sundays and again at two a.m., for the insomniacs. The telephone rings halfway through the Lacrimosa – well, I'll put it off and pick up again when they're repeating it next Thursday. This is not what culture should be about, and so I'm not in favor of cable.

Seriously, what can the new technology offer to the twenty-first century symphony orchestra? Judging from the past and the deteriorating present, very little, except for these few developments discernible over the past twenty-five years.

There are those who argue that the aesthetics of television presentation are hostile to the appreciation of music. Bad television is certainly no friend to symphonic music, but good television, by which I mean sympathetic television done by people who care about music and know a bit about it, is a definite addition to the way we can perceive music. Television concerts are not, I plead with you, the icing on the orchestral musician's cake. I urge managements to take time with television concerts, to realize those concerts are ambassadors to the outside world. They require money and time for rehearsal. Don't allow conductors to assume that because the orchestral players know the piece, somehow cameramen and vision-mixers can learn it just like that without having the chance of playing the piece through before seeing it.

Television can bring the symphony orchestra on a human level into the home, introducing the orchestra to people in a way not possible in any public forum. Television can do things no other medium can do; it can combine pictures and music in a way that isn't possible in a concert hall. The medium is a basis for essays. It has a potential for teaching. I would urge all orchestra managements to collaborate with television, not to believe that big names are passports to good television programs.

The London Symphony Orchestra is working with us on projects with Michael Tilson Thomas, which have taken weeks to plan and develop. The Philharmonia is doing a program on the history of the requiem with the BBC, so that's three or four programs a year, on composers as brilliant as Takemitsu, Stravinsky, Benjamin Britten and Mahler. In Vienna, Bernstein has worked on essays on Shostakovich. In Scotland, the BBC worked with the Royal Philharmonic Orchestra and a young fiddle player named Isaac Stern to develop the notion of spon-sorship in the field of television in a way more vital and creative than usual. The Scottish Gas Board, Isaac, or was it the Tourist Board – no, the Post Office – paid for you to fly to Orkney, to give the first performance ever of Peter Maxwell Davies's new Violin Concerto, which you had commissioned. We are devel-oping an understanding of music, going beyond simply saying, 'Here's Beethoven's Sixth Symphony, enjoy it!' There is more than one public.

It is discouraging to read the audience reports, which portray the people who watch BBC Television concerts as over the age of twenty-five and probably female. And yet Simon Rattle has been on the cover of the *Radio Times*, which is seen by twenty million people. We were disappointed that the audiences who watched the program about John Adams of California were only 0.5 per cent, but half a million people is five Wembley Stadiums. We've stressed contemporary music, but through television we can help people enjoy all kinds of music better.

We hope that this half a million people is the audience of the future.

As a practical proposal, resulting from our time here, John Rushby-Smith and Hans Landesmann both offered interesting suggestions. We could help to make an important series with Pierre on twentieth-century developments in music, or create a lobby for radio and television to go out and meet symphonic orchestras and their managements. That we haven't spent a lot of time talking about it isn't to say that there aren't many, many ways of doing it. Please forgive me for my rather long dissertation. I hope I've given some food for thought.

Audience Education

ERNEST FLEISCHMANN: More than a dozen years ago, Zubin Mehta gave great offense to the good people living in southern California. He made it clear in an interview that he did not enjoy conducting concerts in their civic auditorium because there were hardly any receivers in the audience. I think we all know what he meant: a lack of musical understanding, of musical perception in his listeners. He pointed up a problem that isn't confined to music but applies to all the arts. Leonard Bernstein, in testimony given in 1977 before the House of Representatives Sub-Committee on Select Education, put it with his customary eloquence, 'We're still victims of our ancient attitudes, regarding the arts as a light diversion, an evening out, a curious office building, a comforting blanket of background music, an occasional BBC play about Richard III on educational television channels, whatever superficially entertaining hour it may be, and we'll always retain these attitudes until we become, not only an art-producing people, but an art-consuming people.... Only a society prepared by education can ever be a truly cultured society.' I would go further and say that only a people prepared through an arts education will truly be able to receive the benefits that our civilization, with its constantly astonishing history, ever-growing store of tradition and its exciting, risky, adventurous bent for experimentation, can bestow upon every one of us. Today I want to make a plea for the kind of education that can prepare us, young and old, to receive the full range and enormous impact of those benefits.

In the USA and elsewhere, an emphasis on arts education remains in spite of many budget cuts. It has been in the actual doing, the making and performance of art, that we've taught young people to be active participants. Indeed, considering the abundance of music, painting, sculpture, photography, short story, play writing and other competitions available to anyone with talent, one could almost imagine that someone out there is trying pretty hard to turn the arts into another arena of competitive sports.

A young conductor I know recently had a guest engagement with a rather good orchestra in a Midwestern town. Conversation at dinner after the concert turned to government funding of the arts, particularly to arts education. 'Why should we be forced to pay taxes to teach kids about music?' demanded one of the members of that orchestra's board of directors. 'Kids should take part in sports; that's natural, that's the American way. Music's not natural. It's something we've got from Europe.' The arts may not be natural because we don't grow up in an atmosphere where the arts are a normal, natural part of our everyday existence. Except in our major cities, it's not easy for Americans to leave home and walk a few blocks, take a streetcar or a bus and go to a museum, concert, play or opera. In Germany, in France, Norway, Holland that can still happen in the cities. It's possible there, if the schools are willing and prepared to help, for children to learn how to enjoy to the fullest, how to truly understand and appreciate what the arts have to offer them. A popular culture, television, pop music, most movies, these are designed to produce easy, instant responses. The arts, however, need to be understood, to be actively perceived in order to produce responses. Responses that are difficult, but yield profound change, rich and strange feelings. Our instant response culture may well be impossible to extinguish but we can and must do everything in our power to provide alternatives, to prevent us from turning into a society of totally desensitized push-button automatons, ready to respond to the most obvious and most superficial of stimuli.

Let's teach art history and music history relatively and practically with living examples. Field trips to concerts and plays should be the end result, not the only exposure to the arts. Sophisticated technology enables us to do for classical music and the visual arts in the classroom what pop records and music videos do at home. We must teach students to listen actively, creatively; to sharpen their aural perceptions. Romanticism must be shown to have its counterparts in literature and the visual arts: where a piece of music is influenced by a work of art or architecture, let's not shy away from making the explicit connection. We should study the Isenheim Altar in Colmar in conjunction with Hindemith's *Mathis der Maler* symphony and examine the mighty architecture of Cologne's cathedral when we ask our students to listen to the fourth movement of Schumann's *Rhenish* symphony. The writings of E.T.A. Hoffman form a vivid counterpart to the music of many Romantic composers, from Berlioz and Weber to Liszt and Schumann. Look at the work of Braque, Picasso and Hockney when hearing the music of de Falla and Stravinsky; more than the libretto of *L'Enfant et les Sortilèges* links the music of Ravel to the writing of Colette. Making connections is an important aspect of education; whether at a relatively sophisticated level for high-school students or basically, at the elementary-school stage.

In high school, we could teach about style and performance, comparing interpretations not only by great living interpreters but by performers at the century's beginning, whose achievements the phonograph preserved. We're producing fine instrumentalists, pianists, string, woodwind and brass players, of great technical facility. They can play faster, louder and obtain wider color range from their instruments than we thought possible thirty or forty years ago. But these amazing technical skills and mad pursuit of the physical and technical aspects of performance are often not coupled with penetrating, profound musical insight. These new musicians have not had the time or the inclination to find a path towards a deeper understanding of their art. This must have its roots in our failure to create an awareness of the history, right from the time when children learn to count and read and write. How wonderful it would be if they learned to read music at the same time they learned to read words. Then they wouldn't only hear but also study the shape, the texture, the happenings of a musical score. What a glorious difference this could make to the depth of their musical enjoyment.

Many of us who are not art educators care a great deal about the work that educators do. We're aware of the immense problem they face in restoring an awareness of art's importance to society's fabric. Those of us who have some responsibility for maintaining arts institutions are much concerned about contributing our share to that process; without a committed, enlightened approach to arts education, the arts will die for want of support and recognition. Educators, artists, administrators and even politicians need to join hands to ensure that the arts have a vital part to play in the future of our civilization.

We at the Los Angeles Philharmonic have placed the education of what Zubin Mehta called receivers very high on our list. We send groups of musicians together with the youth concert's conductor into the schools and prepare children in the classrooms, by familiarity with the conductor, the musicians and the music, to attend concerts. For our older, high-school audiences, we have special concerts at which we play sophisticated programs, mainly of twentieth-century classics, conducted by major conductors, where a dialogue takes place between audience and conductor. We publish a monthly magazine for our subscribers, dealing with the less familiar music that they are going to hear, suggesting records to listen to, books to read in preparation for those concerts. An hour before every concert we have a discussion, a lecture, a demonstration about that evening's program. These discussions are attended by up to a thousand people at a time, four times a week. There's an enormous hunger for a greater perception. We hold workshops in various art forms every morning during the summer at the Hollywood Bowl. We send music mobiles, which are VW vans with instruments, tapes and charts, out to the schools for demonstrations. We spend our funds not just making concerts but holding workshops and discussions. The educational activities cover a wide variety, for people from the age of six to eighty-six. Orchestras need to get involved in this very actively; we can and must constantly try to do better. Without the active support and cooperation of educators, politicians and administrators, we can't do anything at all. By working together, arts institutions and art educators can achieve many times the sum of the individual parts in this scheme of things, which is one way we can hope for survival.

CHRISTOPHER BISHOP: I was asked to talk here about the London orchestra scene, but may I first say how very much I enjoyed Humphrey Burton's talk – stimulating because it had new ideas. I shall immediately start talking to Nicholas Snowman about the possibility of putting up a screen. That's the sort of brilliant idea which Humphrey would have. Many, many years ago, he and I played piano duets together. There was a kind of subliminal brilliance about Humphrey then; I found the program the other day – the first piece was Handel's *Arrival of the Queen of Sheba*, the second was Bach's *See What His Love Can Do* and the third was Walton's *Duet for Children*. The sequence of those three pieces was a piece of brilliant program planning.

You've all heard quite a lot about my proposed subject, so I shall tell you a bit about London, because it is a peculiar circumstance, and also about contemporary music and the problems we have there. I am afraid contemporary music is a problem throughout the world. There are four self-governing orchestras in London, probably the only ones of status in the world. The first, begun in 1904, was the London Symphony Orchestra. They've all become self-governing to get away from the tyranny of the conductor or entrepreneur or impresario who founded them in the first place. London has the highest attendance per thousand population of any city in Great Britain, which I suppose is what you would expect; the second is Birmingham.

The advantage of a self-governing orchestra is that we have no union problems whatsoever. There are no fights between management and the orchestra, because the orchestra is the management. The managing directors are engaged by the orchestra, by the councils, the boards of management, and they basically have to do what they're told. I have to be careful what I say with the ex-chairman of the Philharmonia sitting opposite me, but they do what they are told, or if they don't do what they're told they try to give the impression that they've been told what they are doing. It is a rather peculiar position.

The players elect their own players themselves, and this is rather a good thing because they tend to elect players in their own image, players they really like, who make the same sort of sound. That is why each of the orchestras has a personality of its own. The Philharmonia string sound goes back quite a long way, in the way that the King's College Choir probably makes much the same sound now as it did in the time of Orlando Gibbons, because of the continued heritage of chorister, teacher, chorister, teacher right down the line. Auditions are very, very tough, taking place periodically when one player has left or moved on or whatever. For a whole year, the new player's membership is provisional; until he makes himself well known, until he makes himself liked, until he gets into the orchestra's way of life, his appointment is not confirmed. When it really is confirmed, as a member he has all the rights.

The London orchestras are all very badly paid. This is the great problem. They work terribly hard in order to earn something in the region of eighteen thousand pounds for a rank and file player, perhaps twenty-five thousand pounds for a principal. Now, that, of course, is horrendous, and in a way gives a lie to there being too many orchestras, if there's enough work for those four orchestras all to do that. But it does put immense pressure on them. It's not as simple as that actually, because the orchestras themselves, the players, are not happy if they're not working. In a bizarre sort of way, they would prefer to be working than to be paid more and not work. This is a particular London itch which I find very disturbing. They don't actually want to be sitting there doing nothing. It is a very severe problem and not one with an easy solution. The status of being in work is perhaps more important than the playing.

There is a very unpleasant atmosphere in London at the moment; I just hope some solution can be found which will be in the service of music. One of our great problems is the performance, because of the financial troubles and because of the very, very small grants we get, of contemporary music. Between September and December this year, only the Philharmonia presented a work of substance by a living composer: Berio's *Sinfonia*. It's as unreasonable to put the full responsibility to resolve this problem on the orchestras, as it would be for them to close their minds to the fact that this problem is particularly acute in London. In a town with only one orchestra, the audience can't be so selective, going to a comfortable classical concert on Thursday if it wants to avoid a contemporary concert on Wednesday. In London, with five symphony orchestras, the audience is spoiled; it can make that choice. The general public don't much like contemporary music, which is a fact we have to face. The symphony orchestras can't afford to sustain the losses they incur if they perform it with any frequency.

Most of us do try to make our programs as interesting as possible, but the Arts Council has a beady eye on our finances, insisting that we reduce our deficits by a third each year – which leaves little room for experiment and adventure. A typical regional orchestra in England – that's not London – receives a grant of forty per cent of its income; the average grant from the Arts Council to the four independent London orchestras represents only about fourteen per cent. Sponsorship accounts for another nine per cent and the remaining seventy-seven per cent of our income has to be earned at the box office. The average European orchestra earns thirty per cent of its income, I believe.

An evening of Beethoven requiring seventy players and playing to a full house may break even. Contemporary composers, however, tend to require a large orchestra, perhaps a hundred. The Berio *Sinfonia* concert I was speaking of, which included Grieg's Piano Concerto and Debussy's *La Mer*, made a loss of 18,615 pounds and the average loss on concerts is 10,000 pounds. The situation is severe. There may be an underlying suspicion that orchestras, or perhaps their managers, who're the people who take the blame, don't really like contemporary music and are only too glad to shelter behind the excuse of financial problems. I don't think this is the case. They don't like the kind of music which makes them abuse their instruments, but orchestras greatly enjoy the challenge of new music.

When money can be found, orchestras and managers respond. During the four years that we were sponsored very heavily by a tobacco company, it was agreed that we could use a portion of that money to put on concerts, called 'Music of Today,' solely devoted to living composers, many of whom were very young. We rehearsed a piece and played it in a performance. The repertoire was selected by a committee: six members of the orchestra, a couple of critics and Simon Rattle. We never played to more than five hundred people – about the average attendance achieved by the London Sinfonietta, which is *the* contemporary music ensemble in London – but the orchestra found the performances enjoyable and stimulating and were very much saddened when the sponsorship ended and the concerts had to cease. I asked the Arts Council whether they would consider supporting the venture, and they refused.

We have performed music by Lutoslawski, Feldman, Lloyd, David Matthews, Finnissy, Copland, Druckman, Knussen, Holloway, Roxburgh, Souster and Ligeti. That gives you an idea of the mix. The prejudice against modern music, particularly if it's suspected of being atonal, shouldn't be underestimated. I have a terrible story to tell: in 1984 Simon Rattle conducted the Philharmonia in a series called 'Mahler, Strauss and their Influence.' One concert, which included a Mahler symphony, began with Webern's *Passacaglia* and Schoenberg's *Five Pieces for Orchestra*. I knew the concert was sold out and was therefore puzzled by the very large number of empty seats at the start. People had deliberately stayed out of the hall to avoid hearing this terrifying modern music – Webern written in 1908 and not actually atonal and Schoenberg written in 1909! After the interval, all the seats were taken for the Mahler. That, I think, is a real horror story.

A critic, reviewing the Berio *Sinfonia* concert a week after, used his opening paragraph to describe how the people behind him had hated the work. It's a hugely enjoyable piece in my opinion and very accessible. Whether it's a great piece, I'm not sure, but the audience listened with pleasure and actually applauded with enthusiasm. People reading the review could be forgiven for thinking, 'Ah, just as I thought; thank God I didn't go,' making a mental note not to go next time Berio – or any other contemporary music – is on the program. Audiences don't want to pay to hear music they've suspected they won't like. But, if they never hear modern music, how will they ever know whether they like it or not? We need to change that attitude if we're going to get out of the rut we're in now.

One way of introducing contemporary music relatively pain-
lessly is to put it into series, a formula which has been used by
various London orchestras. This method, skillfully marketed,
would be very effective, but it tends to suggest that music of
our time is something apart, not for everyday. At the time,
some critics pointed out quite rightly that our 'Music of Today'
concerts had just this fault, pushing modern music into a
ghetto. Music of our time used to be included in normal concerts; if it's worth playing, it's worth comparing with other
good music. On this principle, Sir Henry Wood introduced new
music into the Proms, a practice followed by his successors, in
particular Sir William Glock. It's worked at the Proms because
of their particular magic, and their magic produces, in a sense,
a captive audience, but it hasn't worked with the BBC Symphony Orchestra at the Royal Festival Hall. Unlike the Proms,
the BBC's Festival Concerts come up against the same problem
of overcomfortable competition, which makes programming
contemporary music so problematical for independent orchestras. The BBC Symphony Orchestra, funded of course by the
BBC, who appear at the present to sustain their losses, can
continue for that reason. All praise to them for that and
the splendid work they do. What is really needed is a radical change in the way programming is done at the Festival
Hall.

    We have to realize that we're here to talk about the funding
of music, not just about how wonderful music is, which, I
think, we all know about anyway. I fully support Mr Rushby-
Smith's proposal; we should definitely try to find money for
making recordings. Recordings are permanent; recordings of
contemporary music can be passed round from person to
person. Once they are in the catalogue, they're extremely
important. It's essential to find money for contemporary music
and for contemporary recording during the period the public
discovers the value of music. The public won't change its mind
quickly. We must all strive to accelerate the change. The
present generation of concertgoers or record buyers may
grumble for a time, but the future generations won't forgive
us if we don't have faith in our own times.

ISAAC STERN: Thank you very much, Mr Bishop. Ladies and

gentlemen, we've heard many astute and thought-provoking observations. The problem now is how to bring these things together and to come to grips with suggestions. It has been particularly difficult for the chair, I must say, to remain as neutral as possible and still maintain some order. Certainly, I have my own views and reactions to many of the problems outlined and know many of them from personal experience, because this has constrained some of the things I've said, or I wanted to say and haven't, I'm going to ask Mr Diamand to take over the chair, and make myself a member of the group, so that I can feel free to speak.

PETER DIAMAND: We've had a number of extremely interesting and highly controversial speeches. Many of you will feel exactly as I do: tempted to answer each one in great detail. As we've been asked by the Wheatland Foundation to discuss problems of the orchestra and to suggest how such problems could be solved or situations improved if funding were made available, we must all wish to comply with this brief: to arrive as quickly and as clearly as possible at recommendations that could be taken into consideration by the Foundation. If accepted or amended, they may allow the Wheatland Foundation, in association with other foundations or other groups interested in the problems of the orchestra, to bring about an improvement. To achieve such resolutions would mean foregoing discussion of anything said earlier in this meeting, difficult as this may be.

I would like to suggest that we discuss briefly considerations that may lead to practical proposals. If we are in agreement with such proposals, I would suggest we form small groups according to interest in the various subjects, to meet tomorrow morning to discuss them in a more detailed form. If these small groups could also arrive at a way to put their findings before the full meeting, we will discuss the proposals during tomorrow morning's meeting, and arrive tomorrow afternoon at conclusions which can be drafted and put to the Foundation. I apologize, to all those who have raised such interesting and provocative subjects, that we are not discussing them now. You will forgive me if I aim for this target: that, as quickly as possible, we reach conclusions. I would like to ask Sir Isaiah

Berlin to give a short summing up of his impressions of what has been discussed up to now.

ISAIAH BERLIN: I'm afraid, Mr Chairman, I'm quite incapable of doing that. I've preserved a welcome silence until now, as the only person here whose claim to be present is extremely dubious, the only person not engaged in making music or interpreting it or organizing it. I thought it more decent to say nothing and listen to others' voices. However, provoked as I am by Mr Humphrey Burton's mention of philosophy, which has been my subject, and still more provoked by the ban placed by the ex-chairman on philosophizing, I intend to defy this and say something. My first remarks will be general; my second remarks, I hope, will have concrete significance in the sense that you invited them.

My first point – and I think a question Mr Burton wanted me to answer – why, given the enormous numbers of musicians produced at present, greater probably than in any previous age, there are so few eminent, distinguished persons who are men of genius. Let me say to this, all theories of the rise and fall of cultures on the whole have proved to be totally unavailing. If anyone tells you they know why there was a sudden eruption of genius in Florence in painting in the fifteenth century and a sudden decline, let us say, at the beginning of the seventeenth, you may be sure that the explanation is not adequate. The same holds for why there was a great rise in German music genius at the beginning of the eighteenth century, continuing until the First World War and after. Why not in Russia, in Spain, in Sweden, in Norway? Why are there Belgian composers of distinction and no Dutch ones? This can be answered where the conditions are more or less the same: explanations in terms of social, technological and cultural influences are not sufficient. Even if you knew all the alleged causes before the effects occurred, you could not have predicted the effects. Such explanations are not explanations. Culture rises and falls in mysterious ways; no historian has ever produced a plausible explanation of the waves and troughs of this particular movement.

The second question that I ask myself, originally raised, I think, by Mr Baechi, concerns the financial consequences of putting on modern symphonic music. There are three ways of getting contemporary music listened to. The first is to introduce totalitarian politics. If you create a totalitarian state, people will want to listen to semi-forbidden music of whatever kind. Anyone in Russia who wants to get away from endless repetitions of Tchaikovsky, Glinka, Glazunov, Kabalevsky, Shebalin, Grechaninov, would be delighted to listen to Nono, Berio or anyone else you like. If you really want to provoke the situation, impose totalitarian methods in which semi-dark music, not forbidden but strongly disapproved of by the authorities, is occasionally performed. This will guarantee outside audiences.

If you reject this particular solution, which I fear may be the case, then of course it's more sober to say that if charismatic personalities, conductors and players of great eminence and popularity, put on these things in their programs, this will attract the audiences. But it is the case that not so very many of these distinguished persons like this kind of music quite enough. Some do, and very much to be praised they are for it, but, broadly speaking, some of them do it partly as a matter of duty and without feeling enthusiasm for what they do, which rarely produces an adequate response from the audience. If these persons can be stimulated to do their duty to contemporary music, it would produce large audiences and a greater degree of contemporary musical culture.

The third method is this. Most people, by the time they're sixteen or seventeen, are formed culturally. What they like at age seventeen, they are likely to like at the age of seventy. There are cases of transformation, of musical revolution, of people who have become converted. Bernard Shaw was converted to Wagner comparatively late in life, and this has happened to a good many people here. Two million people in England looked at the television presentation of the famous Boulez Bayreuth *Ring*. A cultural phenomenon of a major order, it is largely responsible for the very full audiences which came to the Welsh National Opera's performance of the *Ring*, which was not all that good and would not otherwise have attracted quite so large a crowd. If schoolmasters in ordinary schools, particularly men of enthusiasm likely to impress the young, could be induced to stimulate love of music and to explain how modern music has arisen; if Mr Fleischmann's suggestions are followed to link that with other cultural phenomena, to explain what the relation is, as he said, from Hoffmann to Hindemith's *Cardillac*, which can hardly be understood without knowing something about Hoffmann; if that could be done, seeds of interest and taste would be planted in young people. I don't think for that you need musicians, strictly speaking. You need amateurs. Music teachers can't do it because they've too much to do of the routine kind. They can't avoid teaching harmony and counterpoint. They can't avoid conducting players in classical music and they should obviously continue to do so. We don't wish to discourage them, but schoolmasters of a musical kind of mind could be given courses in modern music that would communicate to them and, via them, to their pupils that particular form of openness and receptivity that would create audiences for contemporary music. This can be done at comparatively small expense and it might have quite fruitful results. After this, I shall hold my peace.

PETER DIAMAND: We have already several practical proposals before us. Before we go into them, I would like to ask whether you have any others which you would like to bring up. Probably superfluously, I would like to remind you that we're speaking of proposals from which the orchestra in general should benefit, proposals that might enable the Wheatland Foundation to be helpful, directly or indirectly.

NICHOLAS SNOWMAN: Two proposals: Christopher Bishop's idea which he spoke about just now, sponsoring recordings from different orchestras around the world, on a special label perhaps. I would add one very important condition: that each recording be accompanied by live performances of the piece in question, which is the usual practice at the moment anyway. We get better recordings out of performances.

The second suggestion embodies a banal, well-known idea, but I think a good one: to have commissions given to as many orchestras as possible for new symphonic pieces which are then passed by different orchestras from one to the other for performance. This happened, I think, for the American

Bicentennial: a number of commissions were shared by different orchestras.

ERNEST FLEISCHMANN: A brief remark on that same subject of recordings. Unless we can first put in place a marketing and distribution organization, I'm skeptical. It's been tried in the United States by Composers' Recordings Incorporated, as well as by New World Records, which were well funded and had the backing of the Rockefeller Foundation. They're still in existence but, except that the recordings are made available in universities and libraries, they did not reach the hands of the general public.

PETER DIAMAND: Aware of the difficulties, I would still like to advocate that a committee be formed, to go into the pros and cons and difficulties referred to, and come to some sort of proposal. I suppose you will all remember Mr Rushby-Smith's proposal, but perhaps he could, in a few words, recapitulate.

JOHN RUSHBY-SMITH: Much water has flowed under the bridge since I made my proposal. Sir Isaiah Berlin expressed much more eloquently than I can the importance of creating an audience for new music. Without new music the orchestra, even with the best will in the world, will ultimately die.

My proposal was that a charitable foundation support the recording of contemporary music, indeed of twentieth-century music as a whole. This could take the form of grants to existing record companies, subject, of course, to stringent supervision. Better still, a new label could be established, complete with its own marketing organization, specifically to issue recordings of twentieth-century music, recorded by performers of the highest international reputation and prestige, and engineered to the highest technical standards.

A lot of very small companies in the field issue recordings of contemporary music, usually played by small and relatively cheap forces, which don't make the market because they're not good enough. They haven't got, if you like, the showbiz connection that such music, if recorded by great artists, would have. A recording of Pierre Boulez himself conducting *Pli selon pli*, which I produced a few years ago for Erato Records, has in fact had quite reasonable sales and become a major addition to the recording catalogue, even though its sales may never reach those that a Beethoven record conducted by von Karajan might achieve.

This is one way of ensuring that composers can continue to write for the orchestral medium. They want to have their work performed and they like to have them recorded; they're going to write for other media if the orchestra is not recording. This is very expensive and the market is not a large one for contemporary music as yet. The setting up of a label could help this if it is given the right cachet.

ISAAC STERN: I have been listening with great care to what has been said in these last two and a half days, and have been somewhat taken aback by the defensiveness expressed. Music doesn't need any defense. It has been here for a long time and will be here for a long time. It is the quality of music making that needs shoring up, understanding and performance. It is as true today as it ever was, and will remain true, that a great conductor can fuse an orchestra as nothing else can, making the musicians proud of their calling, adding pleasure to their work, bringing excitement to the creation of music.

I was led to consider these problems, about ten years ago, by the quality of the performances I heard as I played around the world with various orchestras, and the attitudes seen in the players, reflected in the quality of the performances, and the huge rise in the defensive mechanisms in the union contract and elsewhere to defend the imposition of the conductor's tyranny. We all know that conductors did ride rather harshly, and often very unfairly, over the backs of the men before the orchestras were well organized; that the place of the orchestral musician was rather precarious; that his income was nowhere near what his training should have given him. But that has all changed with the increase in the season's length and the amount of money earned. The income for orchestral musicians of established orchestras has risen dramatically: in many countries they are amongst the higher paid of any profession. It is a small profession and one of great honor. Most musicians do feel, at the beginning of their lives, that they are special people given a special role; they have enthusiasm, the fire in the belly, the desire to be musicians.

I began to think about what happens to them when they become members of an orchestra, two or three years down the line – and why does it happen? The problems that we've enunciated all revolve around one central theme: the ability of someone with knowledge and faith to communicate to others that belief, that they too will believe. I don't feel that any part of the music which we have a role to play, should try to pretend to be a better-educated version of popular entertainment and search for an audience. We are part of the leading edge of the human spirit, which is always the narrowest edge. I am perfectly willing to live with that, and see no need to reach for the star status of a pop singer or a movie star – nor do many of my colleagues. We are content to be musicians because it feeds us and gives us strength, and we in turn give others strength. An artist doesn't go out to find an audience. You stand on stage and say 'Come and listen to me.' Any artist worth anything brings his audience to him. You don't try and market him like a packet of bacon.

There's a subtle area of music making – those of you who play will understand what I mean – what bow speed to use, what part of the bow, when and where, differently in Mozart than Brahms, in Stravinsky or Haydn, from the loud noises of Wagner to the delicacies of Debussy. There are different vibratos, there are different uses. These very sensitive nuances must be basic to all music making. I do not agree that any musician who plays well, really well, Mozart, Beethoven, Brahms and Bach, cannot play any form of contemporary music. On the other hand, if you put a piece of Mozart in front of many musicians who play contemporary music, in two measures they are dead. They are making sounds, they are not making music.

Music is ancient, untouchable magic that occurs only at that one moment in life when it is made. Recordings and television can, at best, only capture one moment of one performance, not what that same artist will do differently the next day, the next night, the next month and ten years later. Freezing that moment in time, with that artist and that orchestra, it can be valid in its own way. But it is not the end, and if that is the totality of one's involvement in music, it's like making love over the telephone. It simply doesn't work that way. The French point of view: 'Now, what can I do? *J'ai oublié le trente huit! Je m'excuse.*'

All these problems, I felt, had to be answered in some way. Another aspect of music making has puzzled me – teachers. Who knows how to teach? How good are the people? Ernest Fleischmann is perfectly right, but the ones who have to be convinced are the school educators, the leaders and then the ones behind that. This is different in every country. In the USA education is not a national function, but a state function; today it is even a city function, and then block-by-block. From one block to another, you have an entirely different school administrator. It is he who has to be convinced that the arts should be included in the educational apparatus. Taking all these things – the performer, the leader, the quality of music making, the educator – what do you come down to? You come down to finding a way to create a fighting force, a crack team that will radiate outwards steadily to fill all these areas with true believers, revolutionaries who will not give up their faith when they hit the open markets. How do you do that?

What I have proposed and thought about and am now in the midst of organizing is, for want of a better title, an institute for advanced performance. Forty-seven of the most talented young people one can find will be invited, people who have just graduated from the leading schools and conservatories, beginning principally with the USA because it has the greatest pool of talent that exists anywhere in the world today. Forgive me, all of you from other countries, but this just happens to be a demographic fact. They will be chosen with great care to fulfill the following outline:

1 They stay not for two weeks or six weeks but for two to three years.

2 They are paid. They are paid the equivalent of what is practically a beginning salary in a fairly good professional orchestra, twenty-five thousand dollars per year. Money given as a fellowship has been nontaxable, which would make this the equivalent of about thirty-eight thousand dollars. Most young people graduate from school without a job; they have

to take a job to live, they don't have private means; they have to settle for the sixth stand, or the eighth, in some orchestra. They'll try and they'll audition and take the best offer that comes along. They come out full of beans, willing to play, excited about making music – and within two or three years that dies down, and the cynicism of the older people in the orchestra begins to get to them, and all of this excitement goes for naught. I propose putting these young people through the most strenuous experience they can possibly have. Everyone of them, if they don't speak another language, should learn one. If they speak another one, they should learn a third. German and Italian are necessary.

3 Every string player, even fiddle player, plays viola. Every string player is to have rudimentary education in wind playing and brass playing, just to know what the other instruments are like. The brass and wind players are to have rudimentary training in string playing. All of them are to attend opera rehearsals with the scores so that they can hear what the human voice does and what happens when the lyric theatre is at its best, so that they can translate back into their work the best of what is possible in music. A permanent musical director, visiting artists – I've spoken to at least thirty world-famous colleagues, and there is not one who has not said, yes I'll come for two weeks, three weeks, as soon as we get started. The young people will get to know the best that the world has to offer in the way of experience and knowledge. I want contemporary composers attached to the group. I want every one of the kids in the group, somewhere along the way, to write a piece and hear it performed, so that they know the act of creativity in the field they're entering. We want them to have a guided informational experience, in architecture, painting, literature, to know the relationship between the music they play and the artistic history of mankind. Each will be permitted to play outside the orchestra only with permission from the central group. They will break up into groups to play chamber music. The soloists will come from the orchestra, and the major idea is that they're together not to give concerts but to rehearse, to study, to play. When the works are ready, concerts will be

played, arranged in areas around New York ending up at Carnegie Hall. But by the time they get there, they will have worked things through, they will have tried them out and come back to rehearse again. They will play and will be taken apart, note by note, skinned alive and then they'll go back and work again. When they finally get out to play for the public, they won't have to stand there and make mistakes for the first time.

What does this all lead up to? I know of no other institution that's quite like this in concept, not in music. You have it in physics, in medicine, in law. It does not exist in music.

This would be the first place that the orchestras, the major universities, the schools could come, saying, we need a resident string quartet, we need a viola player. Do you know the difficulties of finding a good viola player today? The Chicago Symphony has been looking for a year and a half and can't find one, at fifty or sixty thousand dollars a year, who meets their requirements. It is the central problem in music: where do you find those raw, young talents that have a chance to come to something? You create this sort of mechanism; you invite them and they try; you pick and you choose, and if you find two out of twenty in the space of five years, you've hit a jackpot. Most of all, at the end of three years, they will know about the life, the real life, of music: they will play everything from Bach to Boulez and will know why they are playing each piece. They'll take the music apart and learn to analyze, they'll learn why every note is where it is, and what their part is in the totality. When they leave, they will be the most informed, the most powerful, the most eager and the most – how shall I say? – undestroyable leaders that can possibly be.

We can't correct these problems overnight. We must be patient, but if we have this program for five years, and at the end of that time if we can find amongst the three hundred people who have passed through ten teachers of great power, we can change the face of music making.

Performances of contemporary music are really not so difficult and blind a subject as one must assume from some of the conversations here. There is a trial period when you perform a composition, to see whether it works or not. If it works and you believe in it, you play it again and again. I speak from personal experience, having played the entire gamut: Prokofiev, Bartok, Copland, first performance of Bernstein; I was involved in the world premieres of Rochberg, Penderecki, Dutilleux, Peter Maxwell Davies. I've had no trouble getting them performed, and when the music is good, other people take it up. That is the final accolade: what others do afterwards.

Other artists now, young people of some renown, are taking up contemporary music because they care for it. It is the performance, over and over again, and a well-prepared performance, that is important. Not just to make do. A performance of a contemporary work should be prepared as meticulously as Herbert von Karajan prepares a Beethoven symphony, and performed at its optimum. The idea of public performance is correct, but with enough rehearsal time. Too often you can get away with a dreadful imitation of a performance of a contemporary work, and nobody knows the difference. Let's be frank about it. Contemporary music has been used as a crutch by many people who are not able to make a career in any other regular way, when those who are really capable – we all know the names, certain conductors, singers, people who are first-rate performers and dedicated to this – do get audiences. There is a truism in music and no amount of support, with the best will in the world, can get away from it.

Hurok was my mentor, one of the last of the great impresarios. He once said, with great truth, 'If people don't want to come, nothing will stop them.' It's true. Our job as performers – the job of the concert managers, orchestral managers, conductors – is to believe in what we're doing and make other people believe in it. As far as young people are concerned, the kind of institute I've outlined recognizes the facts of life in the concert world as they exist; young people going out to it should not go blindly, but armed with knowledge and experience and personal passion. It's the one way we can begin to turn some of this ennui into another path.

PETER PASTREICH: I'd like to propose funding be sought for the study of the orchestra as a workplace, analyzing the problems that exist for the musicians in order to encourage their greater involvement and satisfaction, hence leading to a more effective collaboration between musicians, managements and patrons. We've heard very contrary things in the course of these last few days about whether musicians do or don't like playing in orchestras, what makes them happy, whether their happiness counts. In almost any other field of endeavor, the expert tools that exist today to delineate the structure of a workplace would be used to look at such issues. They should be applied to the contemporary orchestra.

KARSTEN WITT: The musicians union in Germany is publishing a survey on these questions; much research has already been done, and is available.

PETER PASTREICH: I hesitate to say at this moment what budget would be necessary to carry out such a study. Certainly, we would want to bring the very best minds to bear on the question.

LAWRENCE FOSTER: The Aspen Institute once devoted a great deal of time to the medical problems of the orchestral player, particularly those related to hearing. Recently, conducting a *Salome* performance, I was much concerned about a very sensitive eighth violist, seated very near a virtuoso timpanist. Orchestral players do, according to many studies, lose their hearing more and more now. This is a crucial point.

ALEXANDER GOEHR: Much of our discussion has a certain unattractive inward-looking air; we are all, one way or another, representatives of the world's richer nations, coping with difficulties that, to some extent, result from fatigue with our great wealth. I'd like to propose to the Foundation that it take a serious interest in the many rapidly emerging orchestras, and their technical problems, in Asia, especially in the People's Republic of China. An extraordinary wealth of talent is evident there; to a great extent they have not been equipped with even the most rudimentary instruments, as was shown so clearly in Mr Stern's film. I know that there are moves in hand and that much has already been done ...

ISAAC STERN: Point of order! In Japan, there is no dearth of instruments, and the growth of musical training in the best sense, openness, has advanced rapidly. China is another story. They have difficulties, but the infrastructure of our music making, concert halls, etc., has never existed there before. However, they're amongst the most gifted of all the Asians in Western orchestral music, since their own music is intuitively closer to ours than is that of other Asian nations. Given ten to twenty years and their extraordinary work ethic, there will be a true Eastern invasion. We don't have to worry about them; they're going to come along.

ALEXANDER GOEHR: They have no instruments to come along with and their infra-structure ...

ISAAC STERN: They're making their own instruments.

ALEXANDER GOEHR: I know, but are they good enough?

ISAAC STERN: Oh! yes, yes. For them at this point, yes.

ALEXANDER GOEHR: That's a very dubious ethnocentric point of view, to say that their instruments, which are not good enough for us, are good enough for them.

ISAAC STERN: Mr Goehr, the instruments that are good enough for us are no longer available to us; they've been priced out of the market by people who are investing in them as objects for buying and selling rather than using.

PETER HEYWORTH: The proposals so far, particularly Mr Stern's, which I go along with absolutely, concern the internal revivifying of the orchestra. On the first day, however, a number of people raised the question of whether the form of the orchestra, which has served so well over the last two hundred years to match all the demands made by composers, is still able to do so without undergoing certain changes. I'm not sure what the Foundation could do to bring about a growing flexibility on the part of the orchestra or to examine that possibility, but it would be sad if we went away without considering it. It's a practical problem, and perhaps there ought to be a pilot scheme with an orchestra prepared, as it were, to undergo the experiment. This was raised by several speakers, but now that we are formulating practical proposals, this question of whether the orchestra can continue in its present-day form, when the demands upon it are becoming more and more varied, has not been raised. How one would set about it is a difficult, technical problem.

KARSTEN WITT: It is of course very difficult to make any proposal for an international initiative in this area because, as we were saying, the conditions are different in every single country. This is the problem. As far as I understood, Mr Stern made a proposal for the USA. A super-Juilliard or ...

ISAAC STERN: No, no, no. A school for musicians, wherever they may be, from whatever country, wherever they play. Each country needs leaders and this plan is to create leadership – informed, knowing, intelligent, capable, passionate, dedicated leadership. It doesn't have to do with nationality, but with music. It's applicable wherever music, an all-encompassing word, not limited to Baroque, Romantic, Classical or contemporary, is played.

ERNEST FLEISCHMANN: I support Mr Pastreich's recommendation, and suggest that an examination of the management structure – meaning by management the involvement of all concerned parties: musicians, music directors, administrators in the operation of our institutions – be included, to provide the greatest form of job satisfaction not only to the musicians but to all in this musical workplace.

PETER HEYWORTH: Is there any reason to suppose that proposals or recommendations put forward are mutually exclusive? I hope not, that we won't come out of this meeting supporting Mr Stern's idea or Mr Pastreich's, but that the foundation will decide (a) whether these things are good and (b) how much money can be put into each directly.

GARY BERTINI: So many things said at this symposium would,

if only developed, printed, summed up and presented to all those who work in the orchestra, lead to examination of the ideas – which might be then expressed in a practically applied project. When the committees meet tomorrow morning, we will find that some of their concerns express themselves in specific proposals, others in an exchange of ideas, while still others will need research. I would ask my colleagues to reduce everything said during these three days to the following five subjects, enumerated not in order of importance but simply as I've been able to concentrate on them.

1 The educating or training of the best orchestral musicians of the future, according to the necessities of the orchestra at the end of this twentieth century and for the foreseeable future.

2 The use of orchestras throughout the world, the role they play and the role they can play. Without being preoccupied by the subjects of earning a living and fighting unions, how can we develop and improve the orchestras of the future?

3 The structure of the orchestra today. Does it need to change? If so, what changes should be made? What is feasible and what is not? If change is possible, how can it be brought about?

4 If we plan to educate the musicians in the orchestra, we have to approach the specific problems of contemporary music and of specialization. Repertoire is part of that subject.

5 The fifth and last point concerns the new media. Do we continue to play in the concert hall as it is today? What are the other means, present and future, to open new venues and new roads for contemporary music?

PETER DIAMAND: Don't you think that this last could be taken care of in a discussion of the orchestra's structure, as was said before?

GARY BERTINI: No, I don't think so. So much has been said about the structure of the orchestra; the study of other formulas of concerts, shape and so on, even architecture, is in itself quite complicated. One further point about the practical application of projects already mentioned: sums have been quoted. If we are an international conference, we must remember that conditions vary widely. In Israel, country that was very recently marshland has been transformed into beautiful kibbutzim, and the desert has been irrigated. A similar transformation has taken place in the field of music. We are fighting under conditions in which a beginning salary of twenty-five thousand dollars, which Isaac Stern mentioned in his well defined and wonderfully thought out proposal, for the young musicians, is something a musician living here could never even dream of.

It is our problem, but many of you have your own local problems. It's something the committees have to consider when speaking about the problems of orchestras throughout the world, keeping in mind how theories may apply in different places. A musician who finishes his training here, and is very good, can, within exactly the number of hours it takes him to get from here by plane to any place in Europe, the United States, South America, go from a salary of six thousand dollars a year to one of twenty-five thousand dollars. We have to think of building a musical life. We are a very musical country, but conditions here are so difficult and so different that what people are talking about is for me like a mirage in the middle of the desert seen from far away in the mountains.

PIERRE VOZLINSKY: Could the Foundation not take the initiative of launching an international campaign, so that information reaches professional circles, for every orchestra to gradually move over to the system of individual service? Without this – as has been clearly shown at our discussions – no functional progress is possible, and the expense of performing contemporary music will become an absolutely insurmountable obstacle.

GARY BERTINI: Mr Vozlinsky's argument, which seems to me of great importance, belongs to the structure of the orchestra, in my list of five points.

ISAAC STERN: I would like to see Mr Humphrey Burton make a proposal to train TV directors, not so much to watch the music but to learn to use the camera as an instrument. We have so often seen music on television ruined by stock shots:

that same line of three horns, right down to the light glinting off them, then the three trumpets – and always the same fingers on the clarinet, without seeing who's playing and very rarely the relationship between the conductor and the first violinist, the concertmaster, which is one of the most important relationships in the orchestra. When the conductor, the soloist, the musician, comes out on stage, he dominates the audience; the viewer, looking at the television, dominates the screen – the psychological order is reversed. Couldn't you devise, as probably the premier expert in music in the world today, a way of training directors to use the cameras? Not to imitate or mimic the score but to be creative, so that the screen comes alive. I can perfectly well see that ten or fifteen years from now, each house will have a television wall with numerous small speakers around it so that there'll practically be a concert in a room in your own house. But until that time, until the television screens are that size, the efficiency of the director is one of the most important aids to music today.

On the subject of piano tuners and piano technicians: it would be absolutely a boon to music everywhere if a fund could be created for two or three not-too-gifted pianists to give up playing the piano badly and be sent for five years to Hamburg to learn how a piano is put together. After that, two years' apprenticeship in a couple of other places, so that in ten years there would be people who could take care of that instrument, at present so badly cared for in most of the world.

KARSTEN WITT: It's difficult for me to decide into which group to go. I don't think it's my problem alone: the initiatives I would recommend would fit into several of them. We have to make a distinction between summarizing and new initiatives to be recommended. For example, I would like to sit together with others who want to think about helping young professionals, including students and orchestral musicians, to develop. Internationally, there are many initiatives – like the Chamber Orchestra of Europe or the New String Orchestra of Stockholm – where young musicians who don't want to go into orchestras right away try to find new ways. In Frankfurt we have a chamber orchestra and an ensemble where they're playing together in an orchestra, too. Institutions can help them; they can have certain very important experiences, such as working with composers on contemporary music, or working with important conductors and artists from other fields to get ideas about projects linked to other arts ... we could think about building up an international ensemble, an academy.

ERNEST FLEISCHMANN: The Wheatland Foundation has allowed us, as their guests here, to take part in probably the most productive and stimulating discussion on the orchestra that's ever taken place. As far as I understood the brief that you've given us, it's to come up with recommendations for improving the situation of the orchestra on a global basis, as it were, rather than with concrete proposals for the Wheatland Foundation to fund. Lord Weidenfeld was quite right to ask us to be very specific, but to come up with recommendations.

GORDON GETTY: We've discussed having five committees in the morning. Youth orchestras and certain other training and educational ideas should go into one committee, under the heading of education of musicians, at whatever age. Programming philosophy might be one committee – to consider contemporary music and its funding as well as, under the same broad heading, the role of media, recordings, television, the superevents that appear, like Boulez's *Répons*: all that is part of the same issue. What kind of music to program and how to get it to the people. The recompense of performers and their workplace conditions, a matter of keen interest, could be a committee in its own right.

GARY BERTINI: To add to those points brought up of piano tuners and television directors: we might consider that tone masters of recordings and radio stations have much to do with orchestral work, and that, with so many halls being built in the world, so few are really successful acoustically. These are problems every musician has to deal with.

PETER DIAMAND: I would agree with you, but I don't quite see what sort of recommendation could be formed. We all feel that we need acoustics, we need piano tuners, but I don't see *prima vista* how the Wheatland Foundation can provide them.

HENRI DUTILLEUX: I wanted to suggest a something that fits in with Mr Bertini's scheme of a moment ago, notably in terms of educating audiences. The audience doesn't travel, the audience with certain concert associations, the public we'd like to create. This is something that could be discussed at these committees.

ISAAC STERN: A quick point, perhaps to be studied by the group that will consider the performance of contemporary music: I've had the experience in London of wanting to play contemporary work and never having enough proper rehearsal time; there is also the problem of so-many-hundred-less seats sold the moment you announce Bartók or Prokofiev instead of Beethoven or Mendelssohn. It would be lovely to have a fund to take up the slack when the ticket sales fall off in individual concerts. How this would pertain to an orchestra that works on a subscription base, I'm not sure, nor how the fund foundation pattern would work out, but these are all areas of worthwhile investigation for the performers of contemporary music.

LILIAN HOCHHAUSER: Two rather basic suggestions: first, many orchestras cannot afford first-class performers. Nothing stimulates an orchestra more than to have a great conductor or a great artist performing at least two or three times a year. The other is that there could be a fund for mounting projects, such as Nicholas is proposing, for pockets within the season: contemporary music coupled with visual art and discussions for orchestras who cannot afford that. It could also be used to draw audiences for performances they could not normally afford.

PROPOSAL: Recording, Video & Audience Development

HUMPHREY BURTON: We met for a couple of hours this morning in room 429 – no doubt it will go down in history as the 429

Resolution. We spent a very enjoyable hour comparing notes about ways to encourage audiences to attend concerts: the old core of what one might call the serious concert goers, subscribers – and it was noted that in some parts of the world this core of serious listeners is falling away – and also young people and people who haven't previously gone to concerts. We had very interesting evidence from Mr Ohnesorg, who runs a big concert hall in Cologne, from Lilian Hochhauser, Ernest Fleischmann and Christopher Bishop, all of whom run concerts in different parts of the world, and from Pierre Vozlinsky on radio and television and the marvellous work done in Paris. We've come up with four suggestions – I hope you might even say, inspired recommendations – to make positive improvements.

We hope that the proposals we're putting forward may indeed inspire the Wheatland Foundation to set up some kind of machinery, an annual survey of possible ways to help in this field, discovering a form of presentation which would allow it to be not merely the catalyst, but an active and regular participator in this field of international developments in the arts. It is more and more difficult to discover sensitive, well-informed organizations to support the arts. First of all then, the question of some form of scholarship, or at any rate teaching method, for directors. We took this up from Isaac's conference suggestion yesterday and we've formulated it as follows:

The committee urges the Wheatland Foundation to inaugurate an annual scholarship for video direction in the field of serious music. Sufficient funds need to be set aside for a musically oriented director to receive specialist training with a national television organization having the stature of Austrian Television Service or the BBC. This to be followed by a period, we suggest three months, of study with a symphony orchestra. For this, funds would have to be made available for living expenses for this bursary holder. Cameras and video recording facilities should be supplied, so that he or she can indeed go round an orchestra, filming different sections, studying how an orchestra looks in performance and in rehearsal. The orchestra should agree to give clearance for nonbroadcast, noncommercial recordings with a study purpose. This demands negotiation, but is by no means impossible. The scholarship holder should have some 'director of studies,' some person to whom he reports, and should be provided with the opportunity to meet senior practitioners, directors and producers and out-standing musicians who have special knowledge of the field of music video – Isaac Stern, Bernstein, Solti, people who've made many programs and who know about the way music works. Of course, two scholarships, three scholarships, a school, would be marvelous, but to stay realistically within the bounds of a not-too-great budget, we would hope to create just one.

Following on from that, our committee proposes the funding of an annual seminar combined with a competition in the field of serious music video. I use this form, serious music video, as it includes classical as well as contemporary music. We must take into account tapes made for distribution outside the inter-national and national television world, made specifically for the video market. So: an annual seminar, with a prize for outstanding works in the field of programs about music of all periods, a second prize to be given specifically for the pres-entation of music written since 1945. I apologize to my col-leagues in the committee: this second prize was invented by Ernest, Christopher and myself, only ten minutes ago. The committee feels that an annual conference of music managers and performers and television producers should be held – in a sense, the kind of meetings we've been having for these last few days. They would provide valuable possibilities and build valuable bridges between the two professions, with the music profession on the one hand and the public, which we try to serve, on the other.

It's further recommended by our little committee that this very place, the Jerusalem Music Center, together with the neighboring Cinemathèque Center, should be chosen if such a seminar could be brought about, as an ideal venue for meetings. We know what a satisfactory atmosphere has been created here, by Ran Evron; we know there are rooms where we can have screenings; the equipment exists: and we think the chance to meet here would be of enormous stimulus to musicians and to music producers in the field of video. Chri-stopher Bishop will make a third proposal.

CHRISTOPHER BISHOP: This proposal originally came from John

Rushby-Smith: namely, to find a way to make gramophone records of contemporary music; to make that music available, in a way it now is not, for people to hear, rather than to read in scores. We suggested that recordings be made either live or in the studio following live performances. If done otherwise, as a specific recording project, the whole thing becomes artificial – and one hopes, of course, to get more live performances.

Now, this has happened before. In particular, the Gulbenkian Foundation put money into contemporary recordings, which were then put out by EMI. EMI was not really interested in those records at all, and they went to the bottom of the heap. In order to succeed where other ideas have failed, we suggested a special label – for argument's sake, you could call it the Wheatland label – to make the records easily identifiable for what they are. The records would be made centrally in all the different countries where contemporary music is performed, and distributed by specialist distribution companies in each individual country – so that you could buy a Wheatland record of contemporary music in any country you visited. This could also be used for mail order, another way of getting records disseminated, which seems to be extremely fashionable and popular at the moment. We don't go to Deutsche Grammophon, we don't go to CBS or EMI and ask them to distribute it, having learned by bitter experience that they really couldn't care less. We make it a special deal.

Of course it would cost money to make the records, and also to distribute them. In the gramophone record industry, which I worked in for fifteen years, the one thing that matters most is a very good distribution network. Otherwise records sit on a shelf, and it costs money to distribute records and money even to keep them in stock. That is a crucial point, which should be covered by any funding. This proposal must be funded in three segments: the performance of the piece will often require financial assistance; the recording itself; and costs of distribution and maintenance of stocks.

ERNEST FLEISCHMANN: Perhaps the first classical music video, and certainly one of the most successful short music documentaries, *Bolero* with Zubin Mehta and the Los Angeles Philharmonic, eventually went on to win an Oscar. It was made as the result of a proposal to the National Endowment Fund for the kind of program that Humphrey outlined. We got funds for a television director who was also a musician, Alan Miller, to spend some months with the BBC in their music department, observing what they do, and then literally to live with the Los Angeles Philharmonic for some two months, to get to know the musicians and learn how the orchestra works. The resultant work was not only successful as a television documentary, but sold in large numbers to schools and for home use. We're not making this proposal out of the blue; it's already been shown to work.

The committee concerned itself to a large extent, as we were asked to, with the development of audiences – a huge term. We observed that the core audience for symphonic music, particularly for the staple, nineteenth-century repertoire, the kind of audience that came to the Israel Philharmonia when Karajan and Klemperer were there, the tailored middle-European audience of immensely knowledgeable listeners who lived for those concerts – this audience is dying out. Because of that, and because musicians are no longer engaged for twenty-six or thirty weeks of the year, but for fifty-two weeks, we've had to search for a huge new audience, not nearly as well informed, not nearly as committed as that wonderful middle-European audience was. Of course, there'll always be an audience for Beethoven and Brahms and Tchaikovsky. But we have had to resort to a variety of means, not only to increase audience size but to develop more committed audiences, to raise the quality of their perceptions, to make them more part of us: a real, active constituency. We looked at a number of the ways in which orchestras are doing this, and came up with the following recommendation. We recommend that a manual be written and distributed, describing a wide range of national audience development projects, designed not only to increase the size of audiences but to heighten enthusiastic commitment to an understanding of the symphonic repertoire, ranging from the eighteenth century to the present day. One or more researchers and writers should be employed to visit orchestras in Europe, the United States and the Orient, to gather information about successful programs. This manual, updated at least every two years, would be made available to music managers everywhere. Including full descriptions of successful musical programs and ancillary activities for audiences of all ages, from schoolchildren to adults, it would also outline market-study results, audience surveys, attendance figures, audience demographics, and incorporate examples of advertisements, posters, brochures and other publications connected with the projects. Local conditions do vary greatly; what works in one city may not work in another. The manual proposed would contain sufficient exciting, practical material to spark the imaginations of those responsible for our orchestral institutions everywhere. Our final goal in making this recommendation is to keep our art form vital, of benefit to the widest and most perceptive possible audience.

PETER DIAMAND: Thank you very much, Ernest. May I thank this committee for the work they have done and congratulate them on the extremely clear, articulate and persuasive presentation made through their three spokesmen. Before we hear the results of the works of the other committees, shall we perhaps discuss what we have heard? Is there anyone of you who would like to make any comments?

HEIN VAN ROYEN: To make only one comment on the third proposal, I would strongly advocate studio recordings made after a sufficient number of performances as desirable. Contemporary music will never be taken seriously if presented only via live performances, which create the impression of a low-budget undertaking. The Donemus Foundation, which has done a lot for Dutch music, has employed this latter system in the Netherlands; inevitably, they have to work with live recordings from haphazard performances. The result is not always good for the sake of today's music.

ISAAC STERN: As a possible addition to the recording of contemporary music, I'd like to raise the question of how scores are chosen, how they are heard before they get into wide distribution. It's so difficult to send the scores around.

Because the studio here is so good, I wanted to offer it to all the composers of this country: if, whatever their music was, they would find a group of musicians, and if the radio would pay the musicians' time for rehearsal, we would offer the composer and that group this studio for as many rehearsals and as long as they wanted. They could rehearse and immediately listen to the rehearsals on tape, rehearsing over and over again until the performance was tuned to the point of proper presentation. We offered to make a tape at that point, one copy of which would remain here in our archives, the other made available to the composer to send to any orchestra or publisher in the world. His work could actually be heard, with the score, in a performance that he himself had prepared. As it's so very difficult for contemporary composers to get their works listened to or even observed by the necessary orchestral managers, conductors and record companies, it would be extremely helpful if something along those lines could be added to this project.

PETER PASTREICH: Yesterday, Chris, when you were speaking in your paper about life in London, you said that your orchestra had performed only one important contemporary work, a piece by Berio, that the other orchestras performed none and that this had to do with the lack of public demand for contemporary music in performance. Could you explain why records of these works would be worthwhile, when performances of them are not?

CHRISTOPHER BISHOP: This is all part of the broader audience education. It's very likely that orchestras are seduced by making records because they get paid. This is a nasty, economic fact. If records are available, it means that managers, conductors and others can actually hear the music, rather than merely looking at a score. Piles and piles of scores are sent in. Unless you have the luxury, which we certainly don't have in London, to employ a specialist to read through them all, masses of them accumulate. It's often extremely difficult to tell what a contemporary score sounds like. The aim is to disseminate the music as widely as possible. Elgar's popularity, for example, would not be what it now is if not for the gramophone; in the early part of the century, his music was almost uniquely known through that medium.

PETER PASTREICH: I don't have the impression that phonograph records of Elgar made him popular.

CHRISTOPHER BISHOP: Oh, no! I think they did. The film that Humphrey Burton made on *Monitor* started the popularity. That records of him were available has certainly increased his popularity – I've seen that happen. If contemporary music is available on record, it is available as sound, and that's extremely important. The very fact that people don't come to concerts is what worries me. With a single performance, you play to an audience measured by the hall, but a record is there for all time. I wanted to try to make a label identified with this, so that if people wish to know where contemporary music can be found, they'll know that this is where to look.

ALEXANDER GOEHR: These schemes are very admirable; I support especially Mr Fleischmann's extremely striking idea. But I do want to say that Mr Bishop, knowingly or unknowingly, is using the classic reactionary argument; one could give many examples in the history of London, and of many other towns, of extremely successful concerts of contemporary music. The message of doom propagated here is not a good weapon to use as a basis for discussion. There are many ways to program contemporary music; some will work in certain circumstances and others won't. Music is a chancy business and always has been. There is no automatic correlation between contemporary music and empty halls. It is a question of bad presentation.

CHRISTOPHER BISHOP: One minute: I think there's a misconception here. I didn't say that because of the empty hall for the Berio, we should make records. Mr Pastreich said to me, in view of yesterday's discussion, how can you imagine that records are going to help? It was not my suggestion. You see the point?

So many divergent issues enter into this argument. We think these records worth making, if at all, for the sake of promoting contemporary music generally, not just for managers and conductors but for the public as well. It's not a didactic argument: we want to make the music of our day generally available, and in our view there is no better way to do this than by the main means of dissemination of music – which is the record.

SEMYON BYCHKOV: When dealing with a piece of music just written, the experience of looking at the score is not as helpful as hearing a tape of it. A recording saves a great deal of time while giving a much better idea of the work. We're not just interested in premiering the piece; we're interested in live performances being given after the initial premiere, and recording is a tool to ensure that many people, many conductors, many soloists will have the opportunity to know the piece and then perform it. This is not the only reason, but one of several.

PETER HEYWORTH: Apart from orchestral managers and their problems with scores, there are all the ignorant critics who can't read scores. We're very grateful when we can get hold of recordings of new or recent music. It really is a help. I must say, however, that I'm absolutely mystified by Mr Bishop's insistence on Elgar as a composer who's been helped by recordings. As far as I know, his first symphony had one hundred performances in the first six months of its life – before there were any symphonic recordings.

JOHN RUSHBY-SMITH: Sandy Goehr said that Bach was helped by the recording industry; so indeed has every single musician and every single composer been helped who's been recorded. However, there's an enormous hole in the repertoire on record – contemporary music – to be filled. It's a great and important and urgent need. We cannot consider that music is properly represented unless all music is available on disc; this is what we think ought to be engineered.

PIERRE VOZLINSKY: A small observation in an attempt to put an end to this British War: that one listens to new works before the composer himself has a definitive vision or impression of it is certainly nothing new. In the history of music, it's impossible to count the number of major works by leading composers that have been rewritten in part or even completely revised after their first airing. You have to accept the risk that if you record a contemporary work in its very first version, it could be radically revised by the composer immediately after the performance. I'm not at all against the suggestion, quite the opposite, but one could allow for a certain time, during which the composer might rethink the work, before the first recording is made, inasmuch as such a recording will then serve as a point of reference.

ALBERT WEBSTER: We all know how expensive the recording situation is; to have an impact, one has to be very wise, allocating what will inevitably be limited resources – at some level less than what we would all hope for. Somehow contemporary works manage to find their way into recordings, but an effective distribution system has been a major, unsolved obstacle; companies and even an orchestra in the United States have tried to deal with the problem. Scores do get translated onto study tapes for managers, conductors and critics to hear; there are organizations like the American Music Center and others throughout Europe; music publishers themselves will peddle those study tapes; but the distribution function is critically important.

GARY BERTINI: I'm fully in favor of that important proposal, but I would like to specify for what reasons we need it. As far as getting information to managers and conductors for further performances, the way described by Isaac Stern is more effective, less costly, and it's enough. A record, a perfect, studio record after performances, is meant for the public. If we consider the process of a work growing in performance, we must simply remember that at a certain moment someone who had the score decided to perform it without the record. The idea that recordings invariably lead to performances is perhaps exaggerated.

Intended for the public, combined with an information center, where tapes – maybe not even of perfect performances but that give the information the way the composer wanted – are available for musicians to listen to, for the general public, for music critics, this project would be extremely useful.

PETER DIAMAND: When the recommendations were made,

surely no one had the illusion that to record every con-temporary work would be possible. Different circumstances have to be taken into account among recordings of live per-formances, specially made recordings, recordings which immediately follow the concert – all of which should be post-poned until the composer feels the work is ready. The rec-ommendations made here contain infinite variety. As long as we all agree that the principle suggested offers great possibilities for the composer and performers and audience involved in contemporary music, knowing that work will have to be done to sort out practicalities, we don't really need to go into details at this moment.

ISAAC STERN: While I think we're all in favor of the basic thrust of this proposal, it may be worth including the major record companies, rather than excluding them, with a grant from whoever will join in this – for two basic reasons. As both performer and as adherent, I find the idea of setting contemporary music aside, away from performances of regular music, less than useful. One continues to play to a small, dedicated group of listeners, rather than attracting others, as can be done when new music is mixed into an overall program, given the same dignity and same approach as the standard performance. A new label, separately made, would tend in the former direction.

Every major recording company will make recordings – provided somebody else pays for them. The cost of making a performance for a special label or for an already existing major label is the same, but the second case has the advantage of an infrastructure already in place, certainly as far as distribution is concerned, depending only on the extent to which the grant includes a specific form of promotion within the company's distribution system. I'm not speaking against the proposal, but for it.

KARSTEN WITT: We use a small label distributed by EMI, and have had quite good experiences with this, as the label is really presented internationally. But on the first point, I wanted to ask a question. I understand this idea of giving directors scholarships to live with an orchestra for a while, but is it not the main problem to find directors who know something about music? Wouldn't it be more important to endow scholarships for interested directors to follow musical studies? Or am I wrong, is this only a German problem?

ERNEST FLEISCHMANN: It probably does not require an extensive musical knowledge on the part of the television director to produce a good program about music: everyone else concerned is there to work with the director. It is terribly important that the separatist theories of television experts, music experts, promotion experts, be destroyed, and that we all work together. An annual conference, where we all get together and profit from each other's experiences and ideas, would probably do more than sending one or two television directors back to music schools. That program takes too long; we haven't time to wait for it.

PETER DIAMAND: I do not know whether the chairman is allowed to disagree but if he were, he would. If I understood Mr Witt correctly, he was not suggesting that the television director be a musician, and be sent back to music school, but that it has been taken for granted that any television expert going into the field of recording orchestral concerts should be musically qualified to such a degree that he could be entrusted with the task.

From the experiences which we, as listeners and viewers, have had with Humphrey Burton's work, we all are spoilt. We know that musical knowledge is an integral part of the television director's knowledge and understanding. We would hope to see this continued.

Let us have a reaction to the recommendation made by Mr Burton: first, to train video and television directors to specialize in music. Who is not in agreement with this proposal? Mr Goehr.

Mr Burton's second notion was that a general, annual seminar, where this kind of meeting could continue, would be fruitful, together with viewings and prizes: one for programs about music and another for presentation of contemporary music. Who is in agreement with this?

MICHAL SMOIRA-COHN: This is an important and valid proposal, but IMZ is doing it all the time; might this not be a kind of multiplication of their efforts?

HUMPHREY BURTON: As a member of the IMZ, I must answer that we did discuss what that organization has already done, but you see, no one expected the conversation we are having to be realistic. Without discussions of this kind, a profile, a target, is much harder to arrive at; they will help to clear the air, to clarify issues. With the support of everybody round these tables saying 'This is a good idea,' it would be possible for me to put the IMZ in a meeting with the Wheatland Foundation and to say: 'Look, we know you already meet in Cannes for four days to look at programs, avant-premieres and so on. The Wheatland Foundation can add to this meeting x-thousand dollars to create a prize, y-thousand dollars to bring managers and communicators together to meet with you people.' Although that seems to be a real possibility, we did not want to waste your time in detailed elaborations at this moment.

PETER DIAMAND: The recommendations made by the committee of which Mr Burton, Mr Bishop and Mr Fleischmann were the spokesmen are accepted by the majority of this committee. Again, I would like to congratulate them, and express my personal admiration for their success in formulating their recommendations in such a clear and inspiring way, which has provoked and will provoke, without any doubt, further discussion.

PIERRE VOZLINSKY: By way of an apéritif, I would like to make three proposals, which I did not discuss with my colleagues this morning for fear that they would steal them from me. The first is to set up a Grand International Competition of Audio-Visual Culture, for the final round, the winner has to recite by heart, and in chronological order, the complete list of Karajan recordings, without stopping and without dying of hunger. The first prize would be a little casket containing all the recordings that Celibidache has *not* made.

My second proposal is that the Wheatland Foundation persuade all the democratic countries to subject their politicians to an examination of musical culture. That seems to me only fair, since a good many of the countries with whom we have excellent relations subject their musicians to a political examination.

The third and – rest assured! – last proposal would be to set up a competition of musical humor in which, after the eliminating rounds, there would be two finalists – obviously, Humphrey Burton and myself – and the first to make the other laugh would be the winner. Of course, that could last many weeks and I would add that it would be necessary that it take place under medical supervision, because I would not wish Humphrey's efforts to refrain from laughing at my jokes to be bad for his health.

PETER DIAMAND: Pierre, I think you may conclude from the reaction to your recommendations that they are accepted unanimously. And, in this spirit, I think we may break for lunch. Thank you very much.

PROPOSAL: Structure & Programming

ALBERT WEBSTER: This committee consisted of Anna Lindal, Richard Baechi, Gary Bertini, Henri Dutilleux, Peter Heyworth, Hein van Royen, Hans Ulrich Schmid, Nicholas Snowman and myself.

It quickly became clear that we intended to focus on music both old and new, but there was a very clear consensus, amounting to a credo, to support contemporary music and to find a way, through structure and programming, to help support contemporary music especially.

Focusing on the future, we spoke about various models, in Los Angeles, New York, the Junge Deutsche Philharmonie, the South Bank in London, the Concertgebouw and others, within the context of the orchestra, and also, in some cases, somewhat outside that context as we know it. We were positive that a new breed of musician is emerging, and that many of those new musicians are within our orchestras. The interest both in various musics and various types of presentation may indeed be coming more and more from interest within the symphony, not imposed by one force or another; there may really be evolution in progress. It was clearly felt that this conference, in addition to providing four days of introductions and friendship and communication of information, might pave the way.

I think all the members of this committee were very much taken by Mr Fleischmann's recommendation for a manual of audience development projects, as there is a synergy between that and our recommendation. It was our feeling that the very best way to deal with all these questions – structure, programming, helping orchestral musicians in terms of performance at both ends of the spectrum – was to gather information, assess it, assimilate it and exchange it. If that team, going forth to collect information, knew there was a possibility to fund exemplary special projects, a good number of projects fitting our purposes would be discovered.

Looking at all these models in more detail, it would become clear that one or more pilot projects should be undertaken, to highlight exemplary situations and help create experimental models that we could all look at in more depth.

GARY BERTINI: The recommendation reads as follows: To assemble information on what has been and is being done, and to expand the orchestra's range of musical activities and programming in light of new challenges confronting it. These challenges are:

1 the individual musician's expectations;
2 new musical requirements throughout the repertoire;
3 the growing diversity of the audience; and
4 the need to develop new and imaginative programming.

This information should be made available to all interested parties. At the same time, it should be evaluated with a view to funding pilot projects. We believe they should take place in different cities, in different conditions, within a certain time span. Such pilot projects offer the most promising approach to meeting the need for a wider range of programming, in which the music of our time will find its natural place.

PETER HEYWORTH: Entering a vaguely charted area, about which too little is known, we were keen to advocate gathering and evaluating information, only then going on to set up a project. Pilot schemes might throw up ways that programs could be made more various, and take into account what is happening in the early field and in the new field. There is no point to funding projects before one is informed.

Of course, collecting information would be expensive. Part of that might be done by ordinary communication on the telephone, but someone would have to visit certain crucial centers to put questions and get detailed information. The primary need in this area is information, and on the basis of that and contacts made and ideas heard, pilot projects would emerge.

Project details are not the real demand at this moment. The information must be gathered first: what is being done, how it has worked; if it hasn't, then why not. Then one can say, we may try this in such a city, or, it might be tried in different circumstances. It would be irresponsible to reverse the order.

GARY BERTINI: What we have in mind is to assemble, in one place, details of what has been tried out, what could not take place because of special conditions, what did take place, what succeeded, what failed, what structures were and can be flexible, which have union problems. We have heard of many projects with many types of ensembles. If all those experiences are put together, we can assess that information and evaluate the sort of pilot project to be initiated. Pilot projects should be developed together with orchestras, both large and small, who declare themselves interested and prepared to remodel a season, or part of a season, to that end. We might decide, for example, to try a certain line of programs in different conditions – from London to a small city in Austria or Germany, in Switzerland or in America – to see how different structures work, to set up varying flexibilities in the orchestra and in the performance of contemporary music, linking programs to other cultural events or not. At the end of the year, we can reach a conclusion, based on how these different pilot projects worked in different places, and know what recommendations to make.

MICHAL SMOIRA-COHN: As a member of the European Broadcasting Union, which for many years tried to create what my good friend, the late Hans Keller, called the European Broadcasting Union Concert Season, I know that a committee there tried to build up a concert season structure, which has now reached a dead end. Somehow all the suggestions brought forth by that committee of experts seemed to be unsatisfactory. They are now looking for new ways to get general attention for new methods of building up concerts. If a committee appeared with a different style program-building project, this could be taken up by the broadcasting unions, who are interested. Under the name of the Wheatland Foundation Concert Program, it could attract great attention.

NICHOLAS SNOWMAN: Without pre-judging the results of research yet to be done, it might be reasonable to throw out the idea that the projects are likely to consist of different forms of concerts.

Conducting live experiments of the ideas already discussed in all the orchestral meetings, we'd have the all-contemporary concert; possibly the mixed formula. We could closely compare all these formulae and examine them and try them out. In city X or Y, let us bring together this symphony orchestra, that specialized Baroque group and this contemporary group; let's put it all together. Let's see if the old pool idea has a future in it – or is it better when everything is kept separate?

The problem with any scientific or other experiment is that you do the experiment and then you think in some senses of what the results are. But let us not forget the experiment that the Orchestre de Paris is carrying out with the Ensemble Inter Contemporain; let us not forget the experiments that orchestras in London want to carry out with other groups. We're talking about looking at those essays in a less empirical way, exploring the whole orchestral world to see what other groups might be interested in, and then proceeding.

KARSTEN WITT: The situation being different in different places, the projects would be different as well. It's therefore possible to make just one concrete proposal. So many people are coming together to say we need more information. This is very important; most of us wouldn't have thought that before. I would point out that there are certain aspects under which this information should be collected. To these two points, I would add that the pilot project itself might not even cost very much money – it could be interesting for the participating orchestras to get this information and advice from the people who are paid to make the programs.

PETER PASTREICH: The second proposal that came on the table from yesterday's committee, made by Mr Snowman, had to do with commissioning works. I assumed that issue would go to this committee, but I haven't heard it addressed. Did you decide that it was not of interest?

NICHOLAS SNOWMAN: The proposition, a very old idea, of course, and nothing new about it, is simple to implement; the round-robin of commissions from the American orchestras in 1977 is a very good example.

PETER PASTREICH: My concern is that if we now vote for this, and we vote for what came out of the education committee, and then we move on to the two other areas, which are far away from composing, we may end up with a final report that leaves the composer almost out of the picture. I think that would be too bad.

ERNEST FLEISCHMANN: Mr Pastreich is quite right in this; I was interested to hear that the committee feels there is a symbiosis between the proposal I made and theirs. There is, however, a fundamental difference: while both would gather information, mine looks for ways to activate an audience, and their recommendation is really an artistic initiative. To make such a plan effective, of acting on research to initiate pilot projects and testing the resultant ideas, as with any artistic initiative, demands an artist at its head. A kind of Pierre Boulez who would be prepared to work in the place where the pilot project is located. This is terribly necessary; that's where a project can pay incredible rewards, and that's where funding will really be required. The gathering of information is not an overwhelming project, but once the information is there, artistic direction is a necessity.

LILIAN HOCHHAUSER: Of course, one always needs an inspired artistic director, but if a project has worked in one country, I see no reason why it couldn't be taken as a model for use in another country. That is certainly the general idea; it wouldn't necessarily take Pierre Boulez to put it into action ... lesser mortals could carry these projects through as well.

PETER HEYWORTH: In answer to Mr Pastreich, we did consider what should be done for composers and individual works, but so many efforts have been made in this sphere, to subsidize this activity or that activity, that we wanted to break out into a new field. We hope to discover whether existing programs can't be revitalized and made to work in a different way, not merely subsidizing a performance of one individual's new work. What Mr Fleischmann says I support one hundred per cent; should we ever fund pilot schemes of the sort proposed, I would hope very much that we would only do so when quite convinced that we had the right people to run them.

PETER PASTREICH: Early in the conference, we said that there was a problem; composers of genius were, for various reasons, looking elsewhere than the symphony orchestra for their creative habits. It will still be difficult for me to accept if in the end nothing results from this conference to help ensure the continuing existence of good composers writing for symphony orchestras. That has a great deal to do with our future.

PETER DIAMAND: At the same time, I wouldn't believe that any tangible suggestions made here would change the minds of those composers who wish to write for symphony orchestras. I may be wrong.

GARY BERTINI: Those questions were raised by several members of the committee, but we decided on purpose to limit ourselves to things which bring those problems – like contemporary music, the writing of music, the proper programming of it – into focus. We discussed every word of the very short recommendation, including the phrase, 'We feel that such pilot projects offer the most promising approach to meeting the need for a wider range of programming, in which the music of our time finds its natural place.' This phrase includes everything that was said by different members of the committee: about commissions, about subsidizing new works, how to include new music, what to do with it and in what way to do it.

ISAAC STERN: To answer the question in another way, if one succeeds in devising a formula that would break open the regular activity of 'the orchestra,' the very fact of excitement and new life in that area would automatically attract composers. They would feel a necessity. I move an acceptance of the proposal as suggested by this committee.

PETER DIAMAND: All those in favor, please raise their hands.

ISAAC STERN: The ayes have it. The motion is passed.

PROPOSAL: Education & Youth Orchestras

JOSEPH POLISI: The members of the Education and Youth Orchestras Committee were Alexander Goehr, Hans Landesmann, Michal Smoira-Cohn, Isaac Stern, Basil Tschaikov and Karsten Witt. The intent of our group was not necessarily to come up with a specific project, but to recommend to the Wheatland Foundation possible areas of potential funding for future applicants. We also realized, very early on, that the question of education and training has threaded itself through the entire conference, related to compositional techniques and approaches to quality of life. I hope to present an accurate summation of a rather abstract topic. The statement is relatively brief; I would urge my colleagues on the committee to add or subtract as they see fit.

Our intent was to formulate clear concepts relating not only to the education of the orchestral musician, but to the quality of life for individuals in orchestras around the world. We agreed that there currently exists an enormous diversity of experience and belief relating to orchestral performance and training. As a result, it was the committee's desire to present a plan of action which could be valid for various countries and situations. We discussed the motivation of orchestra members as an educational matter related to lifelong learning. It was our strong belief that music can remain vital and alive for those members throughout long careers, but they must possess both the techniques of orchestral performance necessary for their craft, and an understanding of musical thought. In this regard, the committee briefly discussed youth orchestras both as the venue for training professional musicians and as a way to educate future audiences, since many members of these youth orchestras do not become professional musicians. It was emphasized that the sense of community, realized by youth orchestras over a period of even three weeks together, instills a love of music and an understanding of the honorable position of an orchestral musician in society.

One of the committee's major assumptions was that although instrumental proficiency must exist to ensure a successful professional life, technical ability must be viewed as only a means to an end: a conscious, creative process of music making. The concept of orchestral self-governance was agreed to be one way to achieve a sense of personal worth and responsibility as a musician and a member of society.

The education of musicians remains the foundation upon which the quality of life of each individual depends. This committee recommends that the Wheatland Foundation explore the possibilities of supporting projects specifically concerned with the education of orchestral musicians. Projects related to the individual needs of different countries, enriching not only the musicians' lives but those of the citizens of those countries, could exist. It is also recommended that the Wheatland Foundation assume a leadership position in identifying and cultivating prominent and knowledgeable individuals within each country, capable of influencing public policy in support of the orchestra as a vital entity. Thus, a worldwide lobby for the needs and future of the orchestra would be created.

ISAAC STERN: These are, of course, very general recommendations; obviously they need to be fleshed out. I don't know whether we can move from generalities to specific pilot projects, but we might arrive at more specifics within the recommendations made so far.

Let me make one minority statement on one small element on self-governance. Certainly, the involvement of the musician in the overall environment is vital, but I am somehow worried by that word 'self-governance'. For musicians to share involvement in the decision-making apparatus is not only worthwhile but necessary. To give that entire apparatus, even in a broken-up form of committees, over to the working body is possible only in a very small group. When you get to a larger orchestra, and certainly when you get to contemporary music, you have to have one captain, to give identity and direction to the whole group. Orchestral playing, at its best, in the large form, as opposed to chamber music, is the result of many parts, the sum of which is greater than any of its parts; and that whole can only be put together by someone of enormous vision, authority and control. It cannot come from the parts of that whole. The democratic principle does not work very well in the final performance of complex music; there you have to decide to cede your sovereignty for the good of the whole. In a way, it's like living in a community where you elect a board of deputies, but find that one person leads and makes the final decision. You may all discuss that decision, but eventually it is the responsibility of one person. Within that context, the musicians' increasing, extended involvement is a practice perhaps occurring more than many of us would like to see. We have all known cases of absurdity when the use of power has become greater than the need.

KARSTEN WITT: Our paper about education is so general because none of us are representatives – nor do we have many representatives here – of conservatories, able to make suggestions on improving the education of students. That was not our aim. Over the past few days we have often discussed the need for more possibilities for professional musicians to improve their ensemble playing, their chamber music, even their techniques and knowledge of these things.

JOSEPH POLISI: I think it was the feeling of the committee – but do interrupt if you feel differently – that, as Karsten said, it was not our role to propose a specific project. Education is indeed an issue, but it does not seem to be, quite honestly, an issue at the technical level – that is to say, how people are playing their instruments – but rather an ongoing process which will continue to enrich musicians as they live in the orchestra. Isaac's point yesterday was a strong and specific one about how that can take place. This is a valid area of investigation in reference to the orchestra; the Foundation should take the recommendation as such.

ERNEST FLEISCHMANN: May I ask Mr Polisi to elucidate what is meant by the specific recommendation that musicians take over the decision-making process? Was that from an artistic point of view, from a planning point of view? I didn't quite understand whether it was in the context of education, performance or general, operational planning.

JOSEPH POLISI: Self-governance was simply the term used to mean that each individual orchestral musician has a musical life within him- or herself; not to suggest their role in programming or picking a conductor, but that they are individuals capable of musical life beyond the organism of the orchestra.

HANS LANDESMANN: That was not even a recommendation. We simply mentioned this problem of self-governance. We want to educate the musicians so that, in cases where it is necessary, they are able and ready to make decisions. I feel very strongly about the recommended worldwide lobby for the sake of orchestras and orchestral musicians. In many countries, the situation we have been discussing for the last three or four days has not come across to the authorities in power; a few individuals, really committed and really interested in this problem, influential enough to make recommendations to governing authorities, should embrace this important cause. Much can be done. Then one can make specific recommendations pertaining to each country's and each region's needs.

PETER HEYWORTH: With regard to musicians taking over the decision-making process: some very unflattering remarks have been made about the London orchestral scene, well justified, I think, since it's one of the scandals of the Western world and has been for a number of years. It was brought about by musicians taking over the decision-making process.

ALEXANDER GOEHR: I think there's a bit of confusion here. This was a committee on education. No recommendations were made that orchestras do or do not govern themselves. We considered the problem of the continuing, inner motivation of orchestral players. We decided that their instrumental ability was not our primary concern as that is *a priori*; we wouldn't be talking about them otherwise. We also talked about the musicians' civic responsibility, to know how an orchestra functions within society, how it is run, how it is programmed, in addition to an understanding of the structure of the music they play. That is all we talked about.

BASIL TSCHAIKOV: As a member of the committee, I had a very strong impression of two main lines of thought. One concerned the musician's preparation, and the second the circumstances manifested once he has joined the profession. That second one was less discussed, because we recognized that other committees were dealing with the structure of the orchestra and reforms there. But the two parts cannot be seen separately. It is no good preparing someone to be an engine driver if you're closing down the railways. If we're preparing people for orchestras in the future, we have to prepare them to be, as we all felt, fully integrated human beings, who use music as a way of fulfilling themselves and who perform an exceedingly important role in enriching the lives within their community. If the circumstances in which they found themselves were unsatisfactory, all that preparation would be valueless.

The two strands go together. The individual questions, such as whether musicians should be self-governing, are quite beyond our control. Social circumstances, economic conditions and many other factors affect in what way, at which place and at what time things are done. We were concerned with the broad view; we wanted the symphony orchestra to continue, to be a place in which musicians could work in dignity, with self-respect and a perception that what they were doing was worthwhile, and that this was recognized by others. They should be prepared by their education to those ends. We hoped the Wheatland Foundation might help in the various ways that come before them in the future: to sponsor any efforts and to assist, politically or economically, with these developments as they arise. That seemed to us a purpose for which the Wheatland Foundation existed, not just a tap to be turned on and off because one had a private desire to follow a particular, well-watered pathway. We considered the organization had set itself much wider parameters. We didn't identify specific tasks, but looked upon our efforts as a way to help the orchestra to continue as the glorious organization it is, by preparing people for the orchestra of the future and by educating them to fulfill that responsibility.

HANS LANDESMANN: This shows how diverse the situation really is. Peter Heyworth referred to the London scene, where he felt that self-government has proved itself inappropriate, but the Vienna Philharmonic, which has been self-governing from the beginning, hasn't been managed too badly and hasn't done too badly. We have to prepare musicians for each eventuality. They may enter the Vienna Philharmonic and then they should be able to add to this very aim, which defines that orchestra.

PIERRE VOZLINSKY: In the course of our discussions, which have already been fairly lengthy, there has been almost no mention of the problem of the conductor, without whom the orchestra is no more than a lifeless instrument. But, if orchestras are to survive – and it's this that is at stake here – it seems to be absolutely vital to reflect on the way in which conductors should be trained, on what they should be as musicians, how to identify people who are capable of becoming conductors and how to give them the means of learning, by successive stages, a profession whose difficulties have clearly escaped no one. In the interests of the discussion and of the repercussions which our discussions will have, I hope that the question will not be ignored.

PETER DIAMAND: I do understand and sympathize with what Mr Vozlinsky has said. I also regret that the role of the conductor, as far as the orchestra is concerned, has been talked about only briefly and rather superficially. It is true that an orchestra without a conductor cannot function, but I think this moment, when we are reviewing the committee's recommendations, is perhaps not the right time to start a discussion about it. We should follow the pattern we have chosen. Unless anyone feels it's of major importance that something more be said on the subject of this recommendation, I would like to suggest that it be read once more, and that we then perhaps get a motion from Mr Stern which can be seconded or not.

SEMYON BYCHKOV: Although I wasn't in that committee, it seems quite clear that they really meant that it's important for young musicians to have the necessary education to cope with this reality, in case they do come into a self-governing orchestra. One hopes to have as little ignorance as possible where major decisions are made. If they don't fall into that situation, such education won't have harmed them anyway. It's of crucial importance, as is evident in the proposal, which I think a very wonderful one.

HEIN VAN ROYEN: I would suggest that we not talk about self-governing orchestras. This is an extreme situation. What would make the life of orchestral musicians more rewarding and interesting is to give them more responsibility in what the orchestra is doing. This does not necessarily lead to self-government.

JOSEPH POLISI: With your permission, Mr Chairman, let me with the members of the committee retract the word self-governing. This was not the idea. We were talking about self-ability, the ability to exist as a musician.

ERNEST FLEISCHMANN: Respectfully, may I slightly disagree with this. I raised this question with a particular purpose. Some extreme opinions have been expressed here, but a most constructive idea has emerged, namely that the education of musicians does include the structure of management, the political structure, the fund-raising structure, as well as at least an overview of programming possibilities. When, and I don't just say if, they're ready to take part in that decision-making process, in which the new musician needs to be involved, and to which he has a great deal to contribute, that he is at least prepared by an enlightened education is of great importance.

ISAAC STERN: Having had experience with orchestras of all kinds, it seems to me the committee has clarified with the utmost precision what they meant. It had to do not with the governing of orchestras' activities as such, but with being involved, by choice, with how and where they could be a part of the musical and, if you wish, quasipolitical direction of the group with which they're involved, so that they do not feel like cogs in a machine, but a vital part of everything that organization does.

On the other side of the coin, which must be seen with great clarity, are the troubles we've all had with orchestral committees. Though precise statistics may prove me wrong, in nine cases out of ten, problems with the unions and the orchestra committee as such haven't originated with the concertmaster or the first oboe, or the first cellist, or the clarinet player, or the timpani player – the key players – but always with the second tuba, the fourth double bass or the double bassoon player. Often the least involved in the day-to-day working apparatus of the organization, they have time to take up the political problems. Most of those involved in the orchestra committees that I've seen were not among the first-chair men. Be that as it may, as a danger signal that lights in my mind when I hear the word 'self-governance,' I point it out.

The primacy of the conductor has been touched on in various discussions over the past few days, the necessary master figure who gives character and identity to a group of individuals. As a solo performer, I'm one of the few who has absolutely no wish to become a conductor, having too much respect for what I think a conductor should be. It is the most complex, the most difficult, the most demanding job – and increasingly demanding as life goes on – in the music world. The conductor has to put it all together and keep on learning. William Steinberg once told me that a young conductor foolishly asked him 'How do you memorize a score?' He looked up with surprise and said, 'I don't memorize the score. I know it.' It is difficult to know a score, and you have to know hundreds of them. You really have to work at being a true master of the craft.

We have a serious lack, as we do in politics, of master conductors to match the increasing number of orchestras and the increasing number of weeks in the season during which these orchestras operate. For one conductor to have the devotion that an Ormandy, or a Stowkowski, or a Szell, or a Reiner, or any of these had is physically impossible today. There's a limit to what one man can do with the number of concerts played. The problem is how to look for and find talents. If a young violinist plays for me, I can tell you within five or ten minutes whether there's a chance that a real talent is there. How it will develop, I can't tell you. With a conductor, you can read all you want; you can study with as many people as you like; you can learn all the hand gestures and you can learn how to analyze a score. Until you've stood up and done it, nobody knows whether or not you have any talent.

I would like to see one phrase added to the excellent report that has been presented: to create within this mechanism of training a possibility for young conductors to come in front of a group of living human beings and start to conduct. Then and only then can you begin to ferret out those possible new talents who are so necessary to the whole body of music. Without them, the music won't work.

PETER PASTREICH: Based on twenty-eight years' experience on the management side of orchestras, I would cite two main reasons that one infrequently finds first-chair players on orchestra committees. The first is that the first-chair players are in many ways the most vulnerable ones. That is, they overscale. Their ability to play with the orchestra depends on the goodwill of the conductor and the manager; they're the least likely to risk that by serving on committees which might have to say things managers and directors don't want to hear. Secondly, they are the ones who get the most satisfaction out of their work. They're closest to the center of power, and are occasionally consulted on important issues of policy in which most of the rest of the orchestra have no voice. Our workplace committee tried to deal with some of those issues.

BASIL TSCHAIKOV: Under the benign and highly civilized chairmanship of Mr Polisi – an example to be emulated by everyone – we adopted a degree of humility that, I must say, I wish could be shown in some other quarters. We didn't think that our brief was to solve the problems of the whole world. We didn't think that we had been asked to discourse on how conductors should be trained, what sort of opportunities they should have, or that we had been given, within our brief, to deal with conductors at all. Nor did we think we were asked to comment on whether orchestras should be self-governing, here, in London, in Vienna or anywhere else. The question of self-governance applied not to orchestras but to musicians. It stemmed from a most interesting development that Mr Witt is engaged in with his orchestra in Germany, in which a number of young players have shown that by their own efforts, with incredible idealism, with virtually no money involved, they can find ways between themselves, by their self-governance, to settle questions of performance, of whether they would play without a conductor, when they would play with a conductor and what sort of programs they would play.

They exercise all those things which we, in talking about how we want musicians to be educated, have been seeking. These people don't only see themselves as instrumentalists, successful or otherwise, but as a group of musicians wishing to serve. And I have to keep on saying what, it seems to me, is forgotten: we play musical instruments, we are managers, we are critics, we do everything connected with music because we are bringing delight to others. This is the point of self-governance: that musicians not just be told what to do, with no chance to make decisions; they might, in the course of their education, learn something about what is involved in governing themselves. Sometimes they would do that under a conductor, sometimes they would do that in a chamber orchestra. There are innumerable ways for human beings to learn to govern themselves within a tremendous range of circumstances. That is what we sought to encompass. A group of people, very diverse and in some ways with opposing aspirations, came together and found a way to resolve this question by saying, 'We don't know what the answers are. All we know is that we want to play some role and ask the Wheatland Foundation to help us.' We want to find a role in which we can help musicians to be better musicians, to be better people, because by being those things, they will be able to serve this art, which we so often talk about, but so infrequently serve.

That is a noble aspiration. It does seem at times that tiny elements are picked on when the grand plan, which is to improve things, cannot be sorted out at once. I shall go away having learned a good deal about how other people think; I don't expect this group to have solved worldwide problems of music and musical organizations, which have defied the best wits of men so far. It would be an impertinence to think we could do that, but I hope we will all go away a little bit enriched by the experience of others; that's what this committee has sought. Thank you very much for being patient and listening to me.

SEMYON BYCHKOV: There is absolutely nothing in what you said that I would disagree with. I welcome it very much, but often one does hear a discussion of musicians and conductors, as if being a conductor implies that one is not also a musician. If we talk about the education of musicians, to the end of better musicians and better people, how can we exclude the conductors? Everything suggested here is perfectly fine; the only problem is that the symphony orchestra will still require a conductor most of the time, and preferably a good one. We can't ignore that there is a problem: even self-governing orchestras need conductors. We have literally hundreds and hundreds of orchestras that require a conductor every day; when they don't get the one that they are excited to make music with, then no amount of special projects, invention of new programming, any of these things will really do the trick. We can't leave this query apart.

PIERRE VOZLINSKY: I'm not going to tell you my life story, but for many years I was simultaneously responsible for two major orchestras, and am responsible for another one at present. Even if I don't know what I'm doing, at least I have a certain experience. This encourages me to put forward a view which will certainly appear reactionary to many – namely that I haven't a moment's patience with the idea that self-management on the part of orchestras is at all efficient. I say this for entirely practical reasons. Decisions that are very difficult to take and which often seem to fly in the face of logic, cannot be taken through the process of majority vote. As a citizen, I am deeply democratic, but I don't think the system of direct democracy can be applied to a group of people as small as that of a symphony orchestra.

I see that I've managed to raise a smile. And so I'll say that this musical pseudo-ecology is bound to end fairly soon in the destruction of high-quality symphonic life. Conductors, music directors and managers must all have the courage to accept their responsibilities, and if they don't succeed in shouldering them, they should give them up. I'll stop now, since I've begun to scandalize you, but not before quoting an author who has already said what I want to say. He's an author whom one shouldn't quote here; unfortunately, and in spite of the fact that he was an extraordinary writer, he built a reputation for being an anti-Semite. I mean Louis Ferdinand Céline. He did write somewhere in one of his letters that 'Collective intelligence requires a superhuman effort.' Not every player is willing to exert that effort.

[The report of the education committee was voted upon and accepted unanimously.]

PROPOSAL: The Orchestra as Workplace

PETER PASTREICH: 'The orchestra as workplace' committee consisted of Lawrence Foster, Catherine French, Frederick Zenone and myself. We'd like to start by thanking the Wheatland Foundation and its staff for bringing us together for what we believe to have been an extremely valuable collaboration.

Our committee perceives that there are major problems which make the orchestra a less than optimal workplace for musicians and administrators, resulting in interpersonal tension and inefficiency of operation, a lack of motivation and often of commitment to the institution. Distrust and antagonism are widespread. Even when artistic standards are high, a sense of disaffection is common. In addition to emotional stress, and perhaps related to it, there is increasing evidence of illnesses associated with playing in symphony orchestras, such as hearing impairment and disorders of the muscles and tendons. All of these factors contribute, we believe, to orchestras operating less effectively and at lower artistic standards and than they otherwise might. So, we propose a study to determine:

1 Morale levels among musicians and administration, using the techniques of industrial psychology to identify the factors which have an impact on morale and to determine whether and how morale affects performance ability. A pilot study involving three orchestras is proposed at a probable cost of around $150,000 – I'm not hesitating today to call this a proposal and to quote prices. Our committee was busy this morning.

2 The prevalence of work-related medical problems and available solutions to these problems. A survey is already being done in the major orchestras of the USA; an analysis of this survey and of other studies and existing data, by the most highly qualified medical experts, is proposed at a probable cost of around $150,000.

3 Possible changes in the workplace, including in the organizational structure of the orchestra, in methods of professional development and in the availability of medical care. Various groups of musicians, administrators and outside experts would study the issues and make recommendations at a probable cost of about $100,000.

The results hoped for by these three proposals are:
(a) that the orchestra will become a more agreeable workplace for musicians and administrators;
(b) that tensions and inefficiency in orchestras will be reduced;
(c) that the orchestra will be enabled to make maximum use of the intelligence, knowledge, energy and creativity of musicians in developing goals for the organizations and pursuing those goals effectively; and
(d) that a sense of commitment to the institutions and a shared

sense of purpose will serve as motivating and directional forces for musicians and administration.

HUMPHREY BURTON: I'm confused. Mr Heyworth thinks that the self-governing London orchestras produce miserable work; this committee appears to think that American orchestras – they were all Americans on the committee – which, on the whole are not self-governing, are also miserable and produce less than perfect work. We know that American orchestras on the whole are run by boards, using a mixture of private and public funds. Is there in fact any link between whether orchestras are managed or self-managed and the quality of their playing? I would respectfully suggest that this has nothing really to do with the way they play, and I have a horrible feeling that the work you've been doing has very much to do with the American world, where psychiatrists talking about your problems form part of everyday life. In Europe, particularly places like Germany and Austria, they haven't got time to go and see the psychiatrist. They're too busy making money.

PETER PASTREICH: I think it's a gross over-simplification to think that the issue is one of structural self-governing or not self-governing. A consideration of whether the orchestra elects a committee to persecute it or whether a board names a manager to persecute it covers only the grossest aspects of structure. There are other possibilities and we think those possibilities need exploration.

HANS ULRICH SCHMID: Perhaps Hans Landesmann can help me in the following statement. Are you aware that the Vienna Symphony has made a study of outside influences on an orchestral musician, such as stress and all kinds of factors that influence them in the orchestra as a working place? Are you aware that there's a book on this that appeared about five or ten years ago?

CATHERINE FRENCH: I know there's been a project underway with the orchestras in Finland for the past four years, with a team of psychiatrists dealing with the relationship of players to their workplace and to the orchestra system. Some of those findings are now being applied to orchestras in Norway and Sweden.

LAWRENCE FOSTER: My participation in this did not concentrate much on psychiatry. Although I'm an American, I've worked in Europe for the last eight years, in Germany and Monte Carlo. To say that European musicians don't have time for discontent or these problems, doesn't seem true at all for the majority of German opera houses, where you find an enormous problem of motivation. I'm not talking about that greatest of all worlds, the Vienna Philharmonic, but when you go to an opera house in Cologne, or even worse, to Darmstadt or Dortmund, where there's a heart of activity, the problem of motivation is enormous. The problems are even worse, I would say, than they are in America. For example, because of peculiar union laws, musicians in Germany cannot do overtime in their own house, but on the same evening, they can go fifty kilometres away and make a full salary for an evening's work. We all know of the troubles of morale over so many years in the Hamburg Opera House, one of the leading opera houses, which was incapable of providing any kind of decent standard.

Certainly this kind of study will have to adapt to the problems of any given country – and each country has its different problems – but there's no implication of self-governing. I agree totally with what Mr Vozlinsky said, but that doesn't mean that one doesn't have to examine the problems of productivity, whether the problems are uncovered and solved by psychiatrists or through research. I wouldn't reject it out of hand.

PETER DIAMAND: Doesn't one get rather the impression that all orchestra musicians are conscripts, who, by some outer force, are brought into a profession they hate thoroughly, which means that they have to be examined by doctors daily as to whether they're mentally, physically, morally able to carry out these tasks? I thought theirs was a self-chosen profession.

LAWRENCE FOSTER: It is, but they don't leave it if they're dissatisfied, that's the problem.

PETER PASTREICH: If I may use an example furnished to me earlier by Mr Zenone. It is very often true for a musician playing in any orchestra that he spends thirty years playing without once being told by anyone whether or not he's doing a good job. This is not something within the experience of most people working in other fields. It's not true of a manager. It's not true of a secretary. It's not even true of most other artists. It must be profoundly demoralizing to live not knowing if anyone cares if you're playing well or not well. That is only one of the many issues that need examining.

PETER DIAMAND: Forgive me, Mr Pastreich, but it has hardly ever happened in any symphony concert I've attended, that the conductor has forgotten to pass the praise he receives on to the orchestra; the audience claps. Few people at whatever work are as used to being applauded, being thanked, as those who appear regularly on the stage, whether musicians or actors. That is hardly lack of recognition.

PETER PASTREICH: I'm talking about individual recognition. That's quite different from recognition of the institution.

JOSEPH POLISI: I wasn't on the committee, but I am American and I guess that puts me in a bit of a hole with reference to this subject. But something concerns me deeply: not even an implicit but a clear insensitivity to the physical and mental needs of musicians in orchestras, which have been researched and looked at very carefully in the United States. That's not to say that it's valid for the medical problems of performing musicians to become a subspecialty of medicine, which almost seems to have happened in that country. What has come out is that soloists as well as orchestral musicians suffer from often severe pyschological and physical problems. The tradition throughout history has been to sweep those problems under the carpet.

Many artists have now come to the fore, saying publicly for the first time that these problems exist. We should not dismiss it as a suspect question, simply because it has not yet been asked in England or France. The enormous pressures on musicians to perform their art have clear psychological and physical manifestations, and to throw this off as if it were some sort of strange phenomenon that perhaps occurs only in the States, is shortsighted.

SEMYON BYCHKOV: A specific problem often occurs, for example, with someone sitting in the last few desks of the second violins, very close to the piccolo player. We have a person in the Philharmonic in Buffalo who is suffering greatly because of the piccolo's high tones. We've tried various shields and all that kind of thing; it's been absolutely horrible because there was a tremendous amount of personal anger between the two musicians. The piccolist still has to perform and a violinist can't afford to go deaf. It happens a lot with people who have to sit very close to the percussion section or close to the trumpets. This should not be ignored. It's just a little example, but the problem is quite common, very serious and very real.

As far as the personal disaffection among the musicians in the orchestra is concerned, I would respectfully suggest that with some orchestras you walk in and know immediately that the musicians cannot stand making music with each other. Yet, walking into another orchestra, where you see that people are very friendly and affectionate, you know there is a chemistry there. They enjoy making music with each other, they get along with each other, and for the conductor it's a tremendous reward. If one would look at orchestras that have problems, one should also look at the orchestras that can speak positively about their experience.

CHRISTOPHER BISHOP: Might I just say that a certain amount of muck has been thrown at the poor old London orchestras, who've managed to survive against much trouble over the years and will continue to survive, thank God. However, I would say that because they're self-governing, because they run their own lives, these sorts of problems don't really apply. I don't mean the physical problems, but they do like working together, and there is a positive attitude. One of the reasons is that, in most cases, they do rule their own lives. In this room there are one ex-chairman of a London orchestra, two ex-managers, and one current one, plus myself. We would all agree, I hope, that an atmosphere of unity and a willingness to work together is produced by an orchestra's self-governing status. I think that's very important.

ERNEST FLEISCHMANN: I couldn't disagree more profoundly. As the longest-lasting manager in the history of the London Symphony Orchestra – and I was only there just under eight years while the orchestra has existed for over eighty – I've observed exactly what Mr Bishop has spoken about – but I've also observed the reverse. It all depends on the personalities of the musicians. It all depends on their interrelationships; it depends on how hard they're working and under what conditions. There is no single norm, no single rule that applies here. The musician in the Gothenburg Orchestra is ready to tear his or her hair out at the conductor's ineptitude, as is the musician in the London orchestra at the ineptitude of his colleague, the second trombone. So many problems, physical and mental, come from working every day with the same group of people, in very tense, stressful situations, with an enormous variety of quality, experience, in an enormous variety of venues, cold, hot, dry, overhumid, resonant, acoustically satisfying. So many things affect a musician's mental state, and there so many ways the physical state can be affected. With all due respect to the chairman, everyone entering into a profession enters that profession with some idea of achieving a certain fulfillment. We cannot blame the musicians that they don't invariably achieve that fulfillment, and we can blame them less than a lawyer or a doctor, for example, because the circumstances of a musician's life are inevitably far less controlled by themselves.

BASIL TSCHAIKOV: Ladies and gentlemen, I've never sought to tell managers, conductors and administrators whether their lives were satisfactory, or whether they conducted their lives satisfactorily, but as a musician of some forty years' standing, I have been frequently told by people who know absolutely nothing about it, whether my life is satisfactory, unsatisfactory, whether I and my colleagues conduct ourselves as we should. As the only person here who has worked under two great dictators – Sir Thomas Beecham and Walter Legge, with both of whom I worked for many years – I must say I worked most happily, had marvelous musical experiences, with both of them. In the case of those with Sir Thomas Beecham, they have been unsurpassed in my life. At the same time, I experienced frustration, aggravation, annoyance and all those other emotions to which as a human being one is exposed.

At the beginning of my life, as a very young man indeed, I worked in perhaps the most extremely self-governing orchestra that there has been in London, namely the LPO during and at the end of the War, under Thomas Russell, an open and avowed communist, who applied to the orchestra all those theories that you'd expect a communist would want to apply. After twenty or so years spent in different orchestras, I finished with another self-governing orchestra. In all of them, I had magnificent, enjoyable experiences and aggravating and dreadful experiences; I wouldn't associate the good things or the bad with the question of self-government. You're all talking about musicians, and I am one of those guys. The people you're talking about, I have lived and worked with for a lifetime, and I assure you that really this whole question of self-governing, which seems to have upset so many people, is irrelevant to our discussion. We're talking about enjoying playing. Why can't we concentrate on things that musicians are actually concerned with? We're not concerned about these other things to the extent that you all are.

PIERRE VOZLINSKY: I don't want to monopolize the discussion, but I've a practical suggestion to make. Could not the Foundation also consider a study of the professional pathology of musicians? We've all noticed that musicians who play certain instruments are exposed to certain unique physical deformities or to specific problems which can be studied. It would be extremely useful to make a study of the social safeguards which musicians or orchestral instrumentalists enjoy in particular countries under particular systems. Harking back to my memories of the radio orchestras – where physical working conditions were often fairly difficult; it's more exhausting in the studio than elsewhere – if, for reasons of professional illness, any musician had to stop performing, even if he was only fifty, he would draw full income until retirement age. This seems a realistic way of looking at things. If everywhere else, in every other system, musicians were safeguarded in this way, the atmosphere in orchestras could be entirely different. At present, a musician with a major physical impediment, who has to give up work often relatively early – unless he can teach, which is not the case with everyone – becomes a sort of social outcast. And that's not acceptable.

ISAAC STERN: A small, querulous voice suddenly made itself heard to me: in discussing everyone's rights, nobody has said anything about the soloist. Not a word. I would like to add a p.s. to your list: that the rights of the soloist be recognized. For rehearsal, they should always have at least twice the number of minutes that the work takes to perform, and the first-chair people should not be allowed to leave during that performance just because they all feel they can play it better. It would be nice to have all the first-chair people present when a soloist comes to visit.

You may want to speak about the hours of work and how many hours are spent in the workplace and to what extent that is pertinent to your enquiry.

FRED ZENONE: Peter has so well determined the hours of work possible. The number of productive hours possible is not finite, not a number that we can go forward with a lantern and look for. If we can manage, however, to make this workplace something to which we all aspire, then the issue of the number of hours would take on an entirely different perspective. As a musician in an orchestra, I'm disturbed to hear in a symposium that would presume to take the symphony orchestra into the twenty-first century, so much conversation that would arrest the symphony orchestra as workplace, and try to keep it in the nineteenth century, ignoring the world of science and expertise. That's appalling.

HUMPHREY BURTON: I was not, of course, wishing to demean the role of science in the future of music in any way whatsoever. Rather than cause the solid weight of the American orchestral force to bear down on me at supper tonight, I'm happy to withdraw and have expunged from the record any frivolity that I may have attempted earlier in the afternoon. I move the vote as quickly as possible.

PETER DIAMAND: Will all those in favor of the motion kindly lift their hands? May I be considered as having voted against?

This, ladies and gentlemen, concludes the recommendations, proposals, observations made by the committees. I would like to thank you all very much. You have worked under very difficult conditions this morning and have achieved a great deal. It is remarkable that you have been able not only to specify subjects which should be put into recommendations addressed to the Wheatland Foundation, but have been able to formulate them in such a way that only certain editorial adaptations will have to be made before they are passed on. I suggest that, once this meeting is over, the Foundation's London office, charged with the preparation of this meeting, formally present these recommendations as the result of our discussions.

I would like to thank very much the Wheatland Foundation, here represented by Mrs Getty and Lord Weidenfeld, for having given us the opportunity to come together here in Jerusalem under such outstandingly beautiful and impressive conditions. I'm sure that I express also your feelings when I say a very warm thank you to the Wheatland Foundation, to Mrs Getty and Lord Weidenfeld.

I would like to add my personal gratitude to Mrs Getty and Lord Weidenfeld for giving me the possibility to invite you all and to bring together representatives of various professions connected with the arts. It doesn't happen frequently that performers, conductors, players, composers, managers, critics and representatives of musicians'leagues can exchange views. I'm very happy that this opportunity has been given to us, and that this discussion took place in such a very pleasant, productive and constructive atmosphere, and that it has led to tangible recommendations.

I would also like to say a sincere thank you to all those who have made our work here particularly pleasant and efficient. The director of the Jerusalem Music Center, Mr Ram Evron, his staff, the Jerusalem Foundation, which has been extremely helpful and gone into all details of our well being here, and I would like very much to thank Belinda Goldschmidt, who has been available and helpful from morning till night.

Last but not least, I thank all of you that you have accepted our invitation to come here; that you have been so involved in the subject of our discussions; that you have participated; that you have given thought to it, not only during the meeting but also on all other occasions, and that you have all contributed largely and generously to make this such a delightful and enjoyable occasion. Thank you very much.

PETER PASTREICH: May we thank the interpreters and the chairman?

GEORGE WEIDENFELD: Ann Getty and I are very gratified to hear, both in statements from the floor and in private conversation, that many of you felt that this has been a worthwhile effort, that new facts and new formulae have been put forward – new even to so experienced and so erudite a group of musicians as we have in this room.

We might say that there were two major parts to this discussion: a diagnostic one and a therapeutic. The diagnostic itself was worthwhile. There may not always be immediate therapy or cures for the ills and complaints, but we believe that the discussion of some of the highly differentiated and nuanced manifestations of these singular problems has led to the clearing of minds and exchange of views, which will themselves be fruitful.

When it comes to those portions of our discussion conducive to action, either philanthropic action like funding, or indeed that of evangelizing, lobbying, or adapting ideas to the daily work, I do believe – and we hope – that something concrete will emerge.

We intend to send you a summary of the resolution of recommendations voted upon today, and to present a considered view of this meeting. We will also send you copies of an edited transcript of these proceedings,because we believe that they could in themselves already be a very important part of what we want to achieve. By having a distribution list of opinion-forming people in the world of music among authorities, governments, etc., we could in fact establish something that may lead to further exploration and elaboration.

I would have thought that the Wheatland Foundation might seriously contemplate two or three possible assignments, either alone or in collaboration with others. There are quite a few others with whom, clearly, we can't compete: UNESCO, the Council of Europe, the monolith of a government or a principality, or one of the great and enormous bureaucratic charity foundations – but we can be a clearing house. We can take individual recommendations extremely seriously. There are two possible areas of action. One is the informational sector. When we have more detail from some of you who stand behind the resolution, perhaps there is more that we can do – certainly produce a book or two on the orchestra, and fund an authoritative, well-informed writer, to reach a wider public. The other area is that of lobbying vested interests and creating platforms. Nicholas Snowman and I are in touch on the South Bank with various international organizations, business firms, governments, with regard to special festivals celebrating the anniversary of a great city or country; this range of contacts might also enable us to mobilize cultural lobbies. I believe that the European Parliament, for instance, is and can be interested in one or two things that came out; I know for a fact that there is one particular point that may strike a very receptive chord.

So, we will be in touch, and I think we will particularly like to keep in contact with the leaders of the various drafting committees, so that if some of your recommendations or proposals prove infectious, we shall be in touch with you.

I thank you very much for this wonderful exchange of views, always lucid, sometimes passionate, sometimes compassionate, and I think most memorable. Thank you very much.